What people are saying about

The Winds of Homecoming

It is rare for me to support a book that I feel confident is truly worth a reader's attention and re-reading. It is beautifully crafted and full of a heart's intelligence. Clearly it comes from years of experience and deep reflection. It will take you to a healing place in yourself and inspire you to live with all your talents and limitations.

Thomas Moore, August 18, 2020, author of *Care of the Soul*

Begin your journey al~ ~~ide Christopher. Dare to share his loss and loneliness anc ... mysterious world of the Divine, t ... e, Teilhard de Chardin and Saint

Sheila Cassidy, June ... *r Laughter, Audacity to Believe* and *Good Friday ...*

Unclouded by Longing

No doubt you've read many books in your lifetime. This one stands out. Christopher's understanding is exceptional. No platitudes or pious restatement of popular wisdom. His insights have been lived and reflected upon and ground to a powder of real profundity. You'll want to read this book, as I have, more than once.

Thomas Moore, July 7, 2017, author of *Care of the Soul*

A moving, deeply moving story that can reveal our woundedness but also our hope.

Jean Vanier, July 7, 2009, founder of L'Arche and co-founder of Faith and Light community

With a wisdom honed by transformative pain, Christopher Goodchild invites us to suffuse our lives with a spacious consciousness from which to engage with what is. A moving, beautiful and profoundly truthful book.

Jennifer Kavanagh, August 7, 2017, author of *The World Is Our Cloister* and *A Little Book of Unknowing*

A Painful Gift

Chris Goodchild's contemplative quest towards becoming at ease with what is, without denying the pain of facing what is in the way of that, is focussed by and within the eternal sky of truth and light.

Marian Partington, July 7, 2017, author of *If You Sit Very Still*

Christopher Goodchild's autobiography of growing up with and coming to terms with his eventual diagnosis of Asperger's is illuminating, particularly in addressing fear of intimacy and entanglement. Few on the autism spectrum tackle this important issue and Christopher does so with great humanity.

Donna Williams, May 7, 2009, author of the international bestsellers, *Nobody Nowhere* and *Somebody Somewhere*

Out of the fires of autistic torment, Christopher Goodchild has produced a wonderful gift of profound, life-giving wisdom for all human beings.

Gerard W. Hughes, October 7, 2009, Author of *The God of Surprises*

The Winds
of Homecoming

Transforming Loss and Loneliness
into Solitude

The Winds
of Homecoming

Transforming Loss and Loneliness
into Solitude

Christopher Goodchild

CHRISTIAN ALTERNATIVE
BOOKS

Winchester, UK
Washington, USA

JOHN HUNT PUBLISHING

First published by Christian Alternative Books, 2022
Christian Alternative Books is an imprint of John Hunt Publishing Ltd.,
No. 3 East St., Alresford, Hampshire SO24 9EE, UK
office@jhpbooks.com
www.johnhuntpublishing.com
www.christian-alternative.com

For distributor details and how to order please visit the 'Ordering' section on our website.

Acknowledgements of permission to reprint previously published materials are on pages 144, which constitutes an extension of this copyright page.

ISBN: 978 1 78904 563 5
978 1 78904 564 2 (ebook)
Library of Congress Control Number: 2020951038

A CIP catalogue record for this book is available from the British Library.

Design: Stuart Davies

UK: Printed and bound by CPI Group (UK) Ltd, Croydon, CR0 4YY
Printed in North America by CPI GPS partners

We operate a distinctive and ethical publishing philosophy in all areas of our business, from our global network of authors to production and worldwide distribution.

Contents

Illustrations

Front Cover *Avenue of Poplars at Sunset*, 1884
    Vincent van Gogh

Previous Titles

A Painful Gift: The Journey of a Soul with Autism.
ISBN 978 0 232 52758 2 *Unclouded by Longing: Meditations on
Autism and being Present in an Overwhelming World.*
ISBN 978 1 78592 122 3

The Winds of Homecoming

Loss and loneliness can cause immense suffering. For many, they can feel like diseases of the soul. However, both loss and loneliness can offer up the raw material from which our interior lives can blossom. Written in the true spirit of the wounded healer, *The Winds of Homecoming* draws from, and is enriched by, the poetry and writings of Rainer Maria Rilke. These fifty short, meditative reflections offer you hope and inspiration to embrace your loss and loneliness, transforming what is limiting and restrictive into something freeing and infinitely expansive. Through his writing, Christopher Goodchild walks alongside us, not in his role of spiritual guide, nor Quaker, but as fellow traveller, writing from a deeply human place of vulnerability. He does not just tell us how to sit in the contemplative fire and be transformed, he shows us. He shows us by the life he has lived... and continues to live. Christopher's latest book, written with his characteristic lyricism and tender-hearted, compassionate observations on the human condition, is enhanced by four evocative woodcuts by Kent Ambler. Allow *The Winds of Homecoming* to guide you home.

To my darling Helen and wonderful son Joseph.

We don't understand that life is heaven, for we have only to understand that
and it will at once be fulfilled in all its beauty, we shall embrace each other and weep.
Fyodor Dostoevsky

Foreword

Although I qualified as a doctor more than fifty years ago and have worked as a psychotherapist, I have never knowingly met someone who was on the autism spectrum. But now I have "met" Christopher Goodchild, and so will you if you read this book.

I suppose what Christopher and I have in common is that we are both what is known as "Wounded Healers". Although my wounds involved a dramatic history of imprisonment and torture, my suffering was relatively short lived. It included interrogation over one night, three weeks in solitary confinement and five weeks in a detention camp.

Christopher's time in "prison", however, stretched over many years. "Given away" as an unwanted baby, he was misunderstood and poorly cared for throughout his childhood. If ever a wounded child needed to be loved it was this one but his loss was compounded by spending eighteen months of his teenage years in a psychiatric hospital.

His story could have grown sadder by the year; he could have ended up homeless or in gaol. But didn't. By some miracle he found God: not the "Gentle Jesus Meek and Mild" but the God of the mystics: of Rilke, Teilhard de Chardin and Saint John of the Cross.

This book is not so much a story as a series of reflections upon loss and loneliness. It took me a while to realise this and to understand the writer. Little by little, however, a picture of the man emerges and one is drawn to love and respect him. I loved him not as a sage nor as a do-gooder but as a man touched and shaped by pain and loneliness and by an ever-closer relationship with the Divine.

I have recently discovered Christopher's little book *A Painful Gift* in which he writes in more detail of his childhood. I have found it a great help in understanding him and recommend that you read it too. Meanwhile, begin your journey alongside Christopher. Dare to share his loss and loneliness and allow it to lead you into the mysterious world of the Divine.
Sheila Cassidy 2020.

Acknowledgements

No sooner had I finished writing this book that my dear friend, Ram Dass, passed away. Ram Dass was without doubt one of my greatest inspirations and guides in the spiritual life.

"We're all just walking each other home," said Ram Dass, and it is with this in mind that I wish to thank my partner, Helen, and my dear friends, Katherine and Brian, who walked with me throughout the writing and preparation of the manuscript for this book.

Thank you to Sheila Cassidy for writing the foreword. The care and attention she has given me has touched me enormously. Her life story has been an inspiration to me.

I am very grateful to Kent Ambler for his four beautifully evocative illustrations which appear inside the book. Rare is it for me to find such a soulful artist whose work touches me so deeply. To more fully appreciate his work, it should be seen in all its glorious colour, which sadly the printing process in this book would not allow.

I would also like to thank Anita Barrows and Joanna Macy for their beautifully evocative translations of Rilke's poetry and for their generosity in allowing me to use so many of them in this book. Also, the other translators whose work has made Rilke's great gifts accessible to us all.

My deepest gratitude goes to Rilke himself, for his profound and soulful poetry which has been an endless source of inspiration to me throughout my life.

And finally, I would like to thank the team at John Hunt Publishing for publishing this book.

Thank you!

Ah, not to be cut off,
not through the slightest partition
shut out from the law of the stars.
The inner — what is it?
if not the intensified sky,
hurled through with birds and deep
with the winds of homecoming.
Rainer Maria Rilke

Introduction

Loss and loneliness can cause immense suffering. For many, they can feel like diseases of the soul; diseases from which there is never hope of finding a cure. However, for some, the experience of loss and loneliness can offer up the raw material from which their interior lives can blossom. Therefore, do not be afraid of loss nor of loneliness, only the not knowing *how* to be with them. Loss and loneliness are both calls for attention. Transforming them can be a lifetime's work, and perhaps beyond this life, yet each little step we take along this journey can be like a homecoming in itself.

Much of my life has been lived on the margins of society as a result of having autism; alienation and a profound sense of loss and loneliness plagued me as a child, causing me to suffer enormously through much of my adult life. Yet today I no longer feel cut off from myself nor adrift from the world. I no longer feel an outsider, more an insider. Still as socially uncomfortable and awkward as ever, this movement from the margins to the centre was not so much a social transformation but an existential and spiritual one. Throughout the book I talk openly and candidly about my own limitations and on-going struggles. I walk alongside you, not in my role as spiritual director, but as a fellow traveller, writing from a deeply human place of vulnerability.

Recently, someone asked me why I feel it is still necessary to refer to autism in my writing. I sense this person felt that autism was somehow a distraction from the spiritual, or that perhaps that by giving it so much importance it diminishes my humanity in some way or another. I don't know. What I do know is that in the same way that a person's colour, ethnicity and sexuality is integral to their humanity, neurodiversity and autism are integral to mine. How can it not be, for it is the lens through which I see the world. However, I do not define myself by being in the autism spectrum, it is simply a *part* of who I am; not *who* I am.

The book was purposely written in the second person, with the exception of the concluding chapter. The reason for this is that the book was conceived spontaneously from many inner-dialogues within myself. Writing in the "you" authentically conveys this gentle offering of guidance from my more expansive Self, to my smaller, more fearful self. This gives the book a loving, tender and parental quality with which I hope you can resonate and make your own.

Each of the fifty concisely written narratives, written in meditative prose, starts with a quotation from the works of the late-nineteenth and early-twentieth-century Bohemian-Austrian poet, Rainer Maria Rilke, whose mystical poetry alongside my Quaker faith has been an endless source of inspiration. The title of this book, *The Winds of Homecoming,* comes from the final line in Rilke's poem, "Ah, not to be cut off". The poem as a whole speaks to me not only of loss and loneliness but also about the longing to be deeply alive, and embracing the depths and vastness of our being.

In Rilke's poetry, in fact in all his work, it is apparent to me that he wrote to affirm his own deepest aspirations. Like myself, and all of us to some extent or other, he was no stranger to loss and loneliness, in fact he feared being consumed and devoured by such experiences. Yet he came to see that in order to live a creative and meaningful existence he needed at least to try and embrace his own suffering, entering into it in a way that could leave him transformed. However, Rilke, like most of us, was flawed, as can be seen from his intense longing and desire for love which he appears to have been unable to fulfil in most of his close relationships, and most tragically with his own daughter.

For me, seeing Rilke's poetic genius in the light of his human weakness does not diminish his gift. On the contrary, I feel it brings it more deeply alive and accessible to us in a way that would not have otherwise been possible. What was expressed through Rilke was undeniably of a higher nature and it is to this exquisite nature that I bow my head in awe. However, these are just words. Like Rilke's poetry, they act as signposts for the journey home to our true and timeless nature, bringing us to the knowledge of things beyond which words can utter.

The Irish poet and author John O'Donohue once said, "A book is a path of words which takes the heart in new directions." It is my hope that this little book will do just that. That you will be inspired to welcome and befriend your loss and loneliness and in so doing transform it into something deeply meaningful for you.

Part One

Ah, not to be cut off

1

Loneliness

Now you must go out into your heart
as onto a vast plain. Now
the immense loneliness begins.

Where did it all begin, this loneliness; this loneliness which has haunted you your entire life?

Loneliness by its very nature resists, so it makes sense that you aspire not to outwit it, but learn from it. When you are able to allow your loneliness to *be*, you cease to be buffeted around by the resistance to it and this in turn creates a space for grace to come through. This is no easy undertaking for you, for in attending and befriending your loneliness, you have had to bear the unbearable agony of loss that is inseparably woven into its fabric. Like a spider's web, each loss you grieve tugs and pulls on the myriad of previous losses within its intricate and delicate structure.

If loss is a cousin of loneliness, then depression is an equally close relative. Yet because of the shame and existential failing associated with loneliness, of the two, depression has been far easier for you to talk about. However, both loneliness and depression seem to feed off each other and together they have brought you to your knees and, at one point in your life, even had you hospitalised.

The more you fled from loneliness, the more it claimed you in some way or other. Fear and terror plagued you like a terrified tiny child who feared the dark, not knowing if the light would ever come again. Yet loneliness has created in you a longing; a longing to connect with your authentic self and a spirituality that reflects this unfolding into the deepest part of your humanity.

Many years ago, you met a Benedictine monk, who once said to you, "What is it that you are most lonely for?" The question, combined with the sage-like manner in which he asked it, disarmed you and opened your heart. The encounter with this hermit changed your life, for it radically challenged your relationship with loneliness. Loneliness, which was historically so laden with shame, now offered a doorway into something beyond what you could have imagined.

In many ways you have come to see that it matters not so much where your loneliness came from, but instead what you do with it. Then, and only then, could your loneliness become the raw material from which your interior life can blossom.

2

Stumbling into grace

And yet, though we strain
against the deadening grip
of daily necessity,
I sense there is this mystery.

Staying open and allowing yourself to be vulnerable changes everything. It does not take your suffering away, but it takes away the resistance to it, and in so doing you are more able to witness your suffering from the perspective of the soul.

Letting go into suffering is by no means over-identifying with it. On the contrary, it is simply working *with* suffering as opposed to against it. Giving in, but by no means giving up. In such moments, and there have been many in your life, you are left feeling as if you have stumbled into grace.

You have had to work hard in cultivating this willingness to be open and staying with the painful lessons that suffering teaches you. And whilst there may be times when it is all just too much and you feel like giving up, deep down you know that there is within you a place where suffering cannot touch you. In such times, when you feel truly beaten, you simply learn to dig deeper. This is beautifully captured by Rilke in his poem, "The Beauty of You":

In deep nights I dig for you like treasure.
For all I have seen
that clutters the surface of my world
is poor and paltry substitute

for the beauty of you
that has not happened yet.

Often it can appear that you are perfectly calm, self-contained and in control. This is an illusion. Autism takes away your ability to adequately communicate non-verbally to the world. You may be screaming inside, but your facial expression and body language will not communicate this. In the past you would cut your arms in a desperate attempt to put on the outside what you felt on the inside. Today, through God's grace and much hard work, you have found more healthy ways of expressing yourself.

Rilke continues:

My hands are bloody from digging.
I lift them, hold them open in the wind,
so they can branch like a tree.

The image here of a tree branching speaks to you of the restorative power of nature and of grace. A grace that carries you through all difficulties, and at times a grace that you just cannot help but stumble into with wonder and awe.

3

Storehouses

Somewhere there must be storehouses
where all these lives are laid away
like suits of armour or old carriages
or clothes hanging limply on the walls.

Maybe all paths lead there,
to the repository of unlived things.

There is within you a storehouse; a place deep within your heart, where all your pain and suffering reside.

As a child you felt like a lone star in the night sky, forever collapsing in upon itself. Alone in a cold and hostile universe you withdrew into yourself. Such intense suffering broke you down; it also broke you open. For in the same way that a break in a piece of pottery can reveal its inner structure, you came to understand what it meant to be truly human by piecing together the fabric of your shattered self. And it is through this integration that you entered the world of grief and grieving.

Slowly you acquired the ability and skill to bear the unbearable pain and humiliation of your childhood. Grieving would eventually turn your perception of yourself upside down and inside out, leaving you with a feeling of complete and utter powerlessness. At times you felt swallowed up and consumed by what felt like an ocean of suffering. That is, until one day you realised that something inside you had died; the person you believed yourself to be no longer really existed. It was a fabrication, sublimely crafted, but not who you really were.

Today you are no longer a lone star, an outsider desperately driven out by your fearful misconceptions of yourself; more of an insider, being drawn out through tenderness and self-compassion. The more you free yourself from the prison of your self-betrayal and limited beliefs, the more you pay homage to that storehouse deep within your heart. So much so that today you enter with reverence this storehouse within, as you would enter a temple. For in the same way that you bow your head to a holy person or sacred image, today you also bow your head to all your costumes, masks and personas which kept you sane.

Your psychological defences kept you safe and protected you when you needed them most. You may have outgrown them, but you will never *dis*own them.

4

The great storm

I am like a flag unfurled in space,
I scent the oncoming winds and must bend with them,
While the things beneath are not yet stirring...
And thrust myself forth and am alone in the great storm.

The very first cool breeze of autumn evokes a memory, not so much in your mind but in your body.

It starts with a tightening in your chest, followed by shallow breathing, agitation and a general sense of impending fear. Then, seemingly from out of nowhere, a mist descends which soon clouds your whole being. Feeling lost and unsafe, you become a mere bundle of muscles contracting and defending itself against life itself.

At first it baffled you, this seasonally-contracted state. Yet slowly, ever so slowly, this "mist" would reveal to you your genesis, your own beginnings in this world. This depressive agitated state dramatically came into being immediately after your son was born. When love came into your life. For this feeling of intense happiness and euphoria was soon to be replaced with overwhelming fear, that someone or something would somehow take him away from you. Such a drama brought into life a near-perfect re-enactment of how you came into this world, when your heroin-addicted mother gave you away for adoption at six weeks old in the mother and baby home.

Over the years you have learned to be with this experience; relating to your pain instead of fleeing from it. You became able to listen deeply and befriend this desperately lonely and terrified little boy within. You learned patience, the kind of patience which is not so much about waiting, but about a willingness to be present; allowing your body to speak to you its unbearable truth. This meant not so much looking away from the trauma, but looking ever more deeply within it; discovering for yourself that which is timeless, unchanging and ever present within the entire drama of it all. In so doing you have come to see that the past and the present are but one. Or as Zen Master and poet Thich Nhat Hanh would say, "Inter-are."

As you write these words you watch the autumnal mist gather and mingle in the air, the sour smell of apples and the damp leafy earth beneath your feet. The intensely colourful leaves fall from the trees, blown in every direction like your restless thoughts: there goes fear, there goes agitation, there goes grief, obsession, overwhelming loneliness... naming each one without getting embroiled in its story.

Gently, you place your hand on the area around your chest. Smiling and breathing into the discomfort you whisper quietly to yourself those famous words from the fourteenth-century anchoress Julian of Norwich:

all shall be well...

5

Embracing struggle

I live my life in circles that grow wide
And endlessly unroll,
I may not reach the last, but on I glide
Strong pinioned toward my goal.

Your disability is both a handicap and a gift. A Painful Gift!

All your life you have been swimming against the stream. Not because you are a glutton for punishment, but because of your autism. Your mind simply processes information in an unusually chaotic way. Unable to sift out extraneous thoughts, feelings, sensations, movements, and sounds, you are easily overstimulated and, as a result, overwhelmed. Your brain just has no filtering system that can process all this information in a clear, coherent manner. Autism also impacts on you enormously in every area of your life, particularly in social interaction. Whilst you are not anti-social, you are most certainly socially challenged.

Depression can be an inevitable consequence of this relentless inner-struggle of endlessly swimming against the flow. Some years ago now, you came across "The Real Work" by Wendell Berry, in his collection of essays, *Standing by Words*. This spoke to you about the truth of not-knowing and that in the spiritual life there are no obstacles on the path, obstacles *are* the path.

Suffering can break your heart, yet it can also stretch it and with that widen your perceptions. "It may be," says Wendell Berry, "that when we no longer know what to do, we have come to our real work, and that when we no longer know which way to go, we have begun our real journey. The mind that is not baffled is not employed. The impeded stream is the one that sings." And sing you do, not in spite of your sensitivity, but because of it. For without such sensitivity you would not be so attuned to your inner-life. *Your* real work is to be mindfully attentive to this inner life and to engage with the world from out of the fruits of such contemplation.

The world may well continue to baffle, perplex and at times overwhelm you, but like in the Old Testament story of Jacob wrestling with the angel, all your struggles in life can with God's grace be transformed into something quite extraordinarily life affirming and meaningful.

There is a time to engage in struggle and a time to let go of struggle. Everything in nature speaks to you of this.

6

Between two worlds

And you know:
he whom they flee is the one
you move toward.

Much of your early life was lived feeling as though you were constantly suspended between two very different and contrasting worlds.

Too autistic for the neurologically-typical world, and too overly-adaptive and emotionally aware for the autistic world, forever it seemed you were floating in liminal space; always on the threshold of these two worlds coming together, yet at the same time always pulling back.

The consequences of living such an unintegrated life were debilitating depression and anxiety. Depression forever hovered above you like a bird of prey waiting to pounce and devour you. However, there came a time when the fear of living a unified life became less than the fear of remaining split off from yourself. That is when integration of these two worlds came about and with it came a grief so overwhelming and all-consuming that you feared being swept away in its volatile undercurrents. Much of the grief was feeling the overwhelming sadness and loneliness of your early life. The sense that you were lost in deep space, so far from home, so far from friends and so impossibly far removed from yourself. Like in *The Little Prince*, Antoine de Saint-Exupéry's meditation on loneliness, which has so many parallels with *your* early life.

Today you live a simpler life which comes from no longer being at war within yourself. You continue to hold tenderly the wounds of separation which often come upon you unexpectedly and without warning. Such as when a beautiful piece of music captures your heart, or the haunting cry of the curlew over the saltmarsh, or the setting of the sun and the turning of the seasons. All these things stretch your heart and widen your perceptions.

You may well be living a more unified life today, but this liminal space, this threshold space within you, remains. It is as though through reconciling these seemingly irreconcilable worlds your woundedness has become a doorway to something much larger than just yourself.

7

An undefended life

I love my life's dark hours
In which my senses quicken and grow deep,
While, as from faint incense of faded flowers
Or letters old, I magically steep
Myself in days gone by: again I give
Myself unto the past: — again I live.

Living an undefended life means living your life with an open mind and an open heart.

You have always aspired to be intimate with truth however much this has been uncomfortable. Recently, you had a DNA test which revealed that the man you were always led to believe was your biological father was in fact not your biological father at all. A big shock after more than thirty years believing otherwise. However, whilst this man may not be your biological father, the deeper truth was that through living as though he was for all these years, a bond was formed between the two of you. A bond that has great meaning and value for you both.

Your earliest experiences in life had a very damaging effect on you. And, as is common with many adoptees and people on the autism spectrum, your sense of belonging and identity has always been precarious to say the least. Forever searching for something you could never quite give a name to, like a refugee, you were constantly seeking and finding refuge, only to then find it becoming submerged, or in some way compromised.

There have been many painful experiences in your life that have resulted in you shutting down and closing off your heart. This is how you survived. Yet to truly live your life you have needed to gently disarm yourself and tenderly befriend those parts of yourself which you had unconsciously deemed unacceptable. In so doing you came to see the painful truth behind those words Hazrat Inayat Khan spoke when he said:

God breaks the heart again and again and again until it stays open.

For you this has involved not just reliving experiences in your head, but dropping ever deeper into your heart. It means feeling the overwhelming sense of powerlessness, vulnerability and despair. It means seeing the great untruth behind all the damaging beliefs which had shaped your very existence. It means holding everything in the light and allowing it all to fall back into the silence from which it came.

Living an undefended life means being intimate with truth, however much this can be uncomfortable.

8

Excuse me sir, I believe...

It's here in all the pieces of my shame
that now I find myself again....
Into them [your hands] I place these fragments, my life,
and you, God—spend them however you want.

"Excuse me, sir," said the eucharistic minister, "I believe you
have something in your pocket."

You were in line to receive Holy Communion when a young
eucharistic minister placed in the palm of your hand the largest
consecrated wafer you had ever seen. Having just started a gluten
free diet you were faced with a rather awkward predicament:
transgress cannon law by just taking a nibble and putting the
rest in your pocket, or just apologise, not take communion, and
return to your seat. You had no time to think. Overwhelmed
and on the verge of panic you simply took what amounted to
your usual amount of the host and placed the remains in your
pocket. When the mass ended and you started walking towards
the church door, the eucharistic minister blocked your path:
"Excuse me, sir, I believe you have something in your pocket,
the host, and I would like you to give it back to me."

So, you put your hand in your jacket pocket and gave her the
consecrated wafer, with all its fragments. Then the minister
asked you to empty out the contents of your other jacket pocket.
Which you did. However, when she asked you to empty out
your trouser pockets as well, you decided you had had enough.
You politely apologised for the whole scene that you had
inadvertently created and informed the minister that you were

leaving.

Over the last twelve years since this event took place, you have told this story many times to friends, family, the parish priest of the church in question, and many fellow Catholics and Quakers alike. Always you retell the story with the utmost sensitivity and respect for the church as well as for the young and enthusiastic eucharistic minister who was simply carrying out her duties on the day.

With each retelling of the story a deeper truth is revealed to you, the most important part of which was how your belief in transubstantiation was now shattered and in pieces, just like the wafer in your pocket. You gave back more than the host to that eucharistic minister that day. You gave back your childhood beliefs.

All your life up to that point, you had ached to believe in the actual Presence, but in this most humiliating of moments a deeper truth came alive in you. As you stood there with all your pockets turned inside out, time just seemed to stop and everything became sacramental. The idea that a man could go through a certain training which could equip him to turn something that was not holy into something that was, seemed like a cruel trick. Your belief in the actual Presence of Christ was not diminished that day. It was simply set free. Free from all restraints. Hence, the movement from Catholicism to Quakerism was born in you. How could Christ, or God for that matter, be any more in your pocket than anywhere else? To suggest otherwise would seem to you almost sacrilegious. To you in that moment, and ever since, everything and everyone was holy. Christ was everywhere. Faith was not something you could possess, but a gift you were now free to receive.

"It is the test of a good religion," said G.K. Chesterton, "whether you can joke about it." And this is exactly what happened when a couple of days later you and the parish priest discussed the whole affair and reflected on it with great tenderness and humour. We agreed to differ on each other's views and wished each other well.

9

An amends to yourself

My God is dark—like woven texture flowing,
A hundred drinking roots, all intertwined
I only know that from His warmth I'm growing.
More I know not: my roots lie hidden deep
My branches only are swayed by the wind.

Your life has been a Painful Gift. Painful, because loss and loneliness have caused you to suffer so much. Gift, because that very suffering, together with God's grace, has opened your heart and expanded your mind.

Loss and loneliness have become the mud from which you have cultivated the flower of love and understanding. And with all this in mind you write this amends to yourself—bestowing unto yourself the same degree of forgiveness and love that you have shown others, as Rilke said, "What goes on in your innermost being is worthy of your whole love..."

As a person on the autism spectrum, much of your life has been spent studying the human condition as opposed to allowing yourself to *be* human. The need to over-adapt as a child had as much to do with being the family scapegoat as it had to do with having autism. At such a tender age you were daily humiliated by your adoptive family for your unconventional and idiosyncratic ways. Rarely a day would pass without being told you were odd, deranged, peculiar and insane. You learned how to act unaffected, as if your life depended on it. Which it did.

Growing up in such a chronically unsafe environment had a very adverse and damaging effect on you. One of the most effective ways in which you survived your childhood was to disassociate yourself from it. But then came the time when you could run no more, only to then spend over a quarter of a century receiving specialist help, remembering all that you had buried away. Beneath all the outrage and betrayal was a loneliness and loss that felt cataclysmic and insurmountable. However, slowly the defences around your heart gave way and the enormity of your suffering was revealed to you through a grieving process that seemed to never end.

You may not have put to rest the ghosts of your past, but you have found a way of befriending them and listening ever more deeply to them. And in so doing you have come to see that the extent to which you can hold tenderly all your sorrows in life, is the extent to which you will not only cease to be defined by them, but freed through them. There is no greater amends you could bestow upon yourself than this.

10

A dignified life

I want to unfold.
Let no place in me hold itself closed,
for where I am closed, I am false.
I want to stay clear in your sight.

Dignity is not something you seek to achieve nor try to keep hold of; dignity is your inherent value.

So easy it is to forget your inherent value, your essential goodness, in a world that is so quick to judge, criticise and condemn you for being odd, unusual or different. As you write these words you reflect on your experience of living in a psychiatric hospital as a young man. Whilst your time in hospital was humiliating and deeply dehumanising, it also gave you insight into the human condition that you would, in all likelihood, never have experienced in quite the same way anywhere else.

In that asylum you learned what dignity was all about, by feeling at first-hand what it felt like to lose it. The inhumane drug treatments that left you feeling little more than a zombie. The sexual abuse and constant anxiety and fear for your physical safety. Your complete and utter sense of powerlessness. Worst of all was the fear that you would be incarcerated and lost forever within its crumbling Victorian walls and walkways.

At night you would look out of your bedroom window and gaze at the stars in the sky. Their beauty and grace lifted your spirits and made you feel you were part of something infinitely greater than you could have possibly imagined at the time. All this was unfolding at the same time as you heard the pitiful moans and cries of the patients immediately below your window. You realised then that, "Joy and woe," as William Blake said, "are woven fine..." Very fine indeed.

Your bedroom window experience in the hospital has stayed with you ever since. It reminds you that the sky is so boundless, that it has no ceiling and that there is nothing that separates you from the starry heavens with all their majesty and grace. It reminds you that suffering and beauty walk hand in hand with each other in this life, and that whenever you forget this, it always comes at great cost.

To live a dignified life for you is to live in the knowing that there is something of indescribable beauty and value within you which can never be taken away by anyone or anything. Living life with such a knowing not only enables you to surf the waves of life more skilfully, it also enables you to plunge into its great depths.

11

Touched by life

My looking ripens things
and they come toward me, to meet and be met.

Your lifetime's work has been to hold tenderly all your suffering and through God's grace transform it into something of lasting value.

It was not always like this. For much of your early life you took flight from your suffering, or perhaps it would be more true to say that suffering took *you*; taking you beyond the place where you could be reached. How then was it possible to come back from such an abyss? To not only survive so many painful and dehumanising experiences, but instead be transformed by them? You have no answer, but Rilke offers at least a glimpse into this area of being "lost and found" in such darkness:

I come home from the soaring
in which I lost myself.
I was song, and the refrain which is God
is still roaring in my ears.

Now I am still
and plain:
no more words.

To the others I was like a wind:
I made them shake.
I'd gone very far, as far as the angels,
and high, where light thins into nothing.

But deep in the darkness is God.

You have found peace from ceasing to search for all the answers as to why you are the way you are. Such an undertaking once had its rightful place, but today it simply gets in your way. What you can say, and you can say it with great conviction, is that life's events, together with God's grace, have touched you into being the person you are today.

It is touch, and being touched, that brings *presence* home. Perhaps this was the true meaning behind the Gospel story in which Jesus washed his disciples' feet. Just like Jesus' disciples, the challenge you face is to integrate and transform this *being touched* into action.

12

You, my own deep soul

You, my own deep soul,
trust me. I will not betray you.
My blood is alive with many voices,
telling me I am made of longing.

How deeply these words of Rilke touch you.

As a person on the autism spectrum you have difficulty with respect to managing your feelings. This difficulty has nothing to do with whether you can feel feelings such as love or desire, but in communicating such feelings in a way that can be understood. Nonverbal communication does not come easily for you, in fact it can be agony for you at times to express yourself. It is with this in mind that the words of William Blake come immediately to mind:

And we are put on earth a little space,
That we may learn to bear the beams of love.

This quotation of William Blake has haunted you ever since you first read his *Songs of Innocence and Experience* as a young man. The fleeting nature of time on earth and the struggle to engage with life with an open heart, drew you ever deeper to his poetry and his life. A life that like yours was made all the richer by a wild imagination and a mystical way of seeing self and the world.

Learning to bear the "beams of love" speaks deeply to you. When your son was born, he beamed with love for you. His radiance cast a light deep into your soul and in so doing brought to light the wound of neglect and lovelessness that characterised your life up until that time. If was as if everything that you had unknowingly hidden away in the shadowlands of your being came mysteriously to the fore.

"Love," said the Indian sage Meher Baba, "is essentially self-communicative; those who do not have it catch it from those who have it." And that is just what happened. Your son's love captured your heart and in so doing infiltrated your entire being and you were changed forever. Through integrating this change into the fabric of your life you came to see that this very love that had been such an agent in your awakening was not actually coming from your son at all, but instead coming through him.

Awakening to love has taken you away from the person you mistakenly believed yourself to be, and mysteriously carried you to a deeper understanding of who you really are. It is here, in this light-filled space, that you can hold, touch and embody what is most real and most true.

Part Two

*The inner — what is **it**?*

13

Thou Art in calm and storm

But I would comprehend Thee
As the wide Earth unfolds Thee.
Thou growest with my maturity,
Thou Art in calm and storm.

There is within you a place of deep knowing, the core of your being, what Rilke referred to as the "Center of all centers, core of cores."

Your attraction to Buddhist psychology and contemplative practice was driven not so much by your desire for enlightenment, but a desire to be free of psychotropic medications. For you longed to feel the wind blowing on your face and your senses fully alive and attuned to the world around you.

For much of your early life, which included a prolonged stay in a psychiatric hospital, you were completely unable to feel your feelings, good or bad, as a result of the effects of medication. From out of this emotional and sensory deprivation was born a longing to feel all your feelings and not be overcome by them.

Through the teaching of the Vietnamese monk Thich Nhat Hanh and with the support of his Community of Interbeing, you have over many years learned to hold tenderly your feelings, using your breathing as an anchor to steady you when the storms of life have threatened to overcome you. This has been no easy achievement and you credit his practice of mindfulness with giving you a freedom that you could not have possibly imagined as a young man.

There are times in your practice when you feel it is getting you nowhere and it all feels in vain. In such times you recall those wise words of Thomas Merton when he said:

you may have to face the fact that your work will be apparently worthless and even achieve no result at all, if not perhaps results opposite to what you expect. As you get used to this idea, you start more and more to concentrate not on the results, but on the value, the rightness, the truth of the work itself.

Meditation is no substitute for living fully in the moment. This is important for you to remember. You practise to help you live. You don't live for your practice.

14

Tenderising of the soul

The angels love our tears... Leaving, they dry our face
with the brush of a wing...

Grief for you has been a painful gift; a long and winding path, paved with tears.

"When the heart weeps for what it has lost, the spirit laughs for what it has gained," goes the Sufi saying. But when you are in the throes of grief it is no laughing matter. For there have been times in your life when you have been truly incapacitated by grief, so overwhelmed and drained by it, that you thought you would never recover, nor wish to. Yet something of infinite value came into being through the surrendering and emptying of yourself into grief. A light was found; a light which can only really be found in the mysterious darkness of grief itself.

Your life has been changed over and over again through grief and grieving. Yet it wasn't always like this. As a person on the autism spectrum who has always suffered with complex mental health problems, you spent the first half of your life running away in sheer terror of your feelings. But then came the time when you could run no more. Exhausted and overwhelmed, you did a complete 180-degree turn and in so doing became completely consumed and over-identified with the very feelings from which you were running.

The movement from denial to over-identification with your feelings felt like an enormous victory at the time, and it was. Yet greater still was the victory that came through embracing deeply your loss and heartache. Such overwhelming loss and unexpressed grief had up to that time shaped and defined you. Rabbi Menachem Mendel of Kotzk, one of the most enigmatic figures in the Hasidic world, touches on this so beautifully, when he famously said, "There is nothing more whole than a broken heart."

Who you really are can only truly reveal itself to you through your brokenness. In so doing, a deeper sense of self and identity can emerge. "God is found wherever He is given entry," said Rabbi Menachem Mendel, "God is found in the broken places."

Grief for you is a painful gift, as it holds the power to tenderise your soul into awakening to itself.

15

By way of loss

Let your flute be still and your soul float through
Waves of sound formless as waves of the sea,
For here your song lived and it wisely grew
Before it was forced into melody.

Loss for you has not been a hindrance to your ability to find joy in this life. For it has been through embracing loss that your life has changed beyond all measure.

However, you have seen many examples in your life of how loss and suffering have destroyed people's lives. No more so than when you were a young man spending eighteen months as an in-patient in a psychiatric hospital. Here you were to witness and experience loss and suffering on a scale that was truly cataclysmic: the loss of sanity, self-respect and, above all, the loss of hope. Only those who have suffered such overwhelming loss are truly qualified to speak with authority without risk of being insincere.

There is a joy that is immune to loss, suffering and the passing of time. Whilst this infinite, boundless joy within may not be always in the foreground of your awareness, it is nonetheless there, like a seed planted in you long before you were even born. All this is beautifully brought alive through the psalm-like prayer by the late George Appleton:

Give me a candle of the Spirit, O God, as I go down into the deeps of my being.
Show me the hidden things, the creatures of my dreams, the

storehouse of forgotten memories and hurts. Take me down to the spring of my life, and tell me my nature and my name. Give me freedom to grow; so that I may become that self, the seed of which you planted in me at my making. Out of the deep I cry to you, O God.
Amen.

This seed of joy was watered early on in your life when you were at Sunday School and were taught the lives of the saints. Then as a young man you were drawn even deeper to the saints, sages and mystics of all the world's great traditions, because they seemed to be more qualified than anyone else in making sense of suffering and transforming it into something of deep and lasting value.

The lives of the saints, sages, mystics and contemplatives continue to illuminate your path. Many of these simple men and women were leading very unremarkable lives, that is until illness or overwhelming loss broke them open, giving them new eyes to see themselves, others and the world around them in such a radically new and loving way.

16

An embodied life

I am not one of those who neglect the body in order to make of it a sacrificial offering for the soul, since my soul would thoroughly dislike being served in such a fashion.

What does it mean for you to live an embodied life? To live as close to your experience as possible?

As a person on the autism spectrum, the world is often an overwhelming place. Sights, sounds, smells, movements, colours and emotions often flood through you like a tidal wave of sensation. When this happens, your mind shuts down a little like a mobile phone does when it prioritises certain key features prior to cutting out completely. However, in living creatively within your limitations, you are able to take heed of the warning signs so as to avoid shutdowns and exhaustion, to be more in the world and less overwhelmed by it. To achieve this, you have to listen deeply and patiently to your body and to what it is trying to communicate with you at any given moment in time.

Much of your life you have lived a disembodied existence. Being so cut off from your feelings resulted in you observing yourself from the outside-in, as opposed to the inside-out. In addition to this, being on the spectrum, you have difficulties with expressing yourself non verbally. For example, you may feel passionately about something, but the way and manner in which you communicate this is often misinterpreted by others. Much of your life has been a struggle to be seen and understood, because so much of what you have been attempting to communicate has simply been lost in translation.

Whilst your mind is often scrambling to absorb and process information, your body by contrast is always in the present moment; it seeks to be nowhere else but in the "here and now". It is for this very reason that your body is such a perfect vehicle and "means whereby" you can be more present within yourself and the world.

You are not here to achieve, you are here to experience; to embody experience. And in so doing your life becomes infused with greater meaning, purpose and depth.

17

As gently as a feather

Then blessed are those who never turned away
and blessed are those who stood quietly in the rain.
Theirs shall be the harvest; for them the fruits.

Much of your life you have been restlessly searching for something you could never quite put a name to.

Busying away the dis-ease within yourself, you became like a rudderless ship upon this ocean of existence. Always on the way to somewhere else, fearing that if you slowed down and felt your feelings, you would be engulfed with unbearable loss and sadness. That is until illness and breakdown created a space for grace and wholeness to flow into you. "If you do not change direction," said Lao Tzu, "you may end up where you are heading." And you know exactly what Lao Tzu meant.

With every depression came an opportunity. A chance to stop and reevaluate your life. Often it felt as though depression had its very own silent centre. A place where you could find refuge and re-learn how to live life on life's terms and not the superimposed life that you previously forced upon yourself.

The greatest change happens within you whenever you can be true to your own experience; training yourself to *be* with what moves within you, as opposed to taking flight from it. This is no easy undertaking.

"Go into yourself..." said Rilke, "Dig down into yourself for a deep answer..."

Often you ask yourself the question, "What's going on, right here, right now?" This question can be a powerful way of bringing your attention back into the present moment. However, you have learned that the effectiveness of this practice is not determined by the frequency in which you ask the question, but instead the quality of love, tenderness and presence which you take into this enquiry:

What's moving within you, right here, right now?

Fear

Courage

Joy

Envy

Hunger   Hope

Thirst

Anxiety

Anticipation

Love

As gently as a feather falls upon a feather, gently return to your breathing each time you catch yourself being distracted, taken away from the present moment.

Attending and befriending yourself in this way helps you to move between the surface and the depths of your being, meeting the drama of what moves within you with greater tenderness and presence...

... as gently as a feather falls upon a feather.

18

What used to be a hindrance

I know that nothing has ever been real
without my beholding it.
You have always had an acute and overbearing conscience; forever
bordering on scrupulosity.

As a child you were haunted with insecurity and plagued with doubts. This often had a religious tone and quality about it. Blasphemous and outrageously offensive thoughts were forever intruding and forcing themselves into your awareness. So convinced that a life of eternal damnation awaited you, unable to eat, drink or communicate, you were hospitalised for the most formative period of your adolescence. It was here you spent your days walking endlessly through and around the grounds and gardens of this crumbling Victorian asylum. You lost your mind. You lost all hope.

Being told you were odd and peculiar by your parents because of your autism simply added an additional layer of anguish to an already wounded and overwhelmed psyche. At times this disease of the mind, with all its irreverent voices and disqualifying thoughts, often left you feeling that you were possessed and teetering on the brink of insanity.

Today there is a name for this "doubting disease"; it is called obsessive compulsive disorder, otherwise known as OCD. Whilst the condition has not left you, what has left you is the shame and stigma that possessed and tormented you in the past. What once drove you out of your mind has now driven you deeper. For you have learned not to get in the ring with this dark beast, but instead to accept your powerlessness over it. In so doing something greater than you moves through you.

In so many ways your story has echoes in the lives of many monks, saints and desert hermits of all the great religious traditions. They too faced great adversity and mental torment, battling with demons that clearly at times had the upper hand. That is until that sublime moment when they realised that freedom came not from out-witting them, but in welcoming them, even befriending them. For in so doing the demons then lost their power and simply fell back into the silence from which they came. "What used to be a hindrance now helps you most," said Meister Eckhart, and how apt those words are in relation to you and obsessive compulsive disorder. For every time you feel the push and pull of this disorder of the mind, it awakens you to ask the question, "What's really going on within you?" For this potentially damaging of conditions simply creates a drama to distract you from a far greater drama that is going on within you that really warrants your attention. Seen in this way, the condition becomes akin to an alarm bell, reminding you to come back to yourself.

In so many ways obsessive compulsive disorder has drawn you deeper into the truth of who you really are, not by rejecting experience, but by embracing it. Always with love, tenderness and a deep desire to really discern that which is true from that which is false.

19

The ear of your heart

Dost thou not see, before thee stands my soul
In silence wrapt my Springtime's prayer to pray?

Each day you take time to sit quietly on your own, in nature or in a church, and read a Psalm or a small reading from the Gospels. You practise not so much to strengthen your beliefs, but to hold them ever more tenderly, experiencing the words as if you were reading them for the very first time.

Listen, my son, to your master's precepts, and incline the ear of your heart.

These opening words in the *Rule of St Benedict* touch you deeply, and how well they resonate with the spirit underpinning the ancient monastic practice of *lectio divina*, the prayerful reading of scripture.

This prayerful contemplative reading of scripture offers you an anchor point in your day. A time when you can drop deeper into the truth of who you really are. Such a practice helps you reorientate yourself, reminding you of your true intention and deeper identity as a soul and child of God.

Each time you practise *lectio*, it is as if you are diving headfirst into the ocean and allowing yourself to be taken by its currents; resting in awareness, resting in "God-ness", as if carried by a piece of music that moves you to the core, inspiring hope, imagination and faith.

The following little piece, taken from *The Way of a Pilgrim*, resonates so powerfully with you with respect to the hidden depths and beauty that can be found in the prayerful reading of scripture:

> *To gain spiritual enlightenment and become a mindful person with an inner life, you must take some text from Holy Scripture and focus your attention and thoughts on it for as long as possible, and the light of understanding will be revealed to you. Do the same thing during prayer: if you wish your prayer to be pure, true and a source of joy, you need to choose some short, simple but powerful words to form your prayer and then repeat it frequently over a long time, and then you will develop a taste for it.*

There is something utterly beautiful when you allow the normal activities of the day to be put aside to rest in God's presence. *Lectio* offers you a doorway into such a presence. To echo the words of Martin Laird, "becoming so silent before God that the 'before' simply drops away. When the 'before' drops away, so do we drop away. We cease to be an object of our own awareness."

20

A radical dependency

I yearn to be held in the great hands of your heart.
Oh let them take me now.

Each morning, before you fully awake; before even your eyes have opened, you gently say the Jesus Prayer:

Jesus Christ, son of God,
have mercy on me...

Although the words of the Jesus Prayer touch you deeply, ultimately it is not the words that really matter. What is of far greater importance is simply setting your intention for the day that lies ahead; handing over your entire life to this power greater than yourself. For there is something far greater than you, working through you. This is not so much a belief, but instead, a radical *allowing* of your life to be shaped and moulded around a deeper reality, beyond the person you believe yourself to be. Perhaps the only real choice you can make in this life is to either accept or reject this "deeper reality" that some people call God.

You fell in love with Jesus not just because he loved humanity so deeply and unconditionally, but because his love came so vibrantly alive for those on the margins of society. Such love opened your heart, first to your pain and suffering, and then to the world's pain and suffering.
"Find the door of your heart," said the Early Church Father St John Chrysostom, "you will discover it is the door of the kingdom of God." So, whilst your mind may well create an

abyss, your heart is always sure to cross it.

The great saints and mystics of all the major world religions are simply mirrors reflecting back to you your true and timeless nature, ever reminding you that you are not the doer of your actions. For it is only through Love that you can be truly free to embrace a life of such radical dependency.

21

Home will bring you home

*I come home from the soaring
in which I lost myself.*

The Winds of Homecoming are rarely gentle, and you never know what events will unfold that will ultimately lead you home.

Rare indeed is there a night that passes without you dreaming of home. Such dreams are often dark, desolate and utterly lonely. A quality of restlessness and agitation underpins these dreams which always in some way or other casts you back into the institutions that shaped your early existence.

You frequently experience what you call *soul sadness*: this sense of being cut adrift from your existential moorings. This creates a deep longing within you; a longing that always draws you ever deeper, for somewhere you intuitively feel you know, yet have somehow painfully forgotten.

There are shadows and echoes of the home for which you yearn everywhere you look, yet to see this you need to stop the desperate searching for it. Then a great release from the pressure of wanting gives way to a very new way of seeing. Home for you is not so much a place or destination, but instead a deep resting; resting into the truth of who you really are. Your thinking mind would have you believe that home is something you can acquire or obtain, but this could not be further from the truth. Rilke enters into this beautifully:

My eyes already touch the sunny hill,
going far ahead of the road I have begun.
So we are grasped by what we cannot grasp;
it has its inner light, even from a distance—

and changes us, even if we do not reach it.

This inner light Rilke talks of is as deep as it is mysterious.

Home will bring you home when you can laugh at your human failings in the knowing that everything has its place in the divine scheme of things. Home will bring you home when your inner authority merges with outer authority; the perennial wisdom that teaches you that ultimately, there is no *where* you need to go to find home. You are there already, you just have not realised it yet.

22

When curiosity becomes stronger than fear

Let everything happen to you: beauty and terror.
Just keep going. No feeling is final.

Often it can feel as though curiosity and fear are in conflict with each other; battling themselves out within your psyche.

When you are able to stop and look deeply you can see that there is no conflict between your curiosity and fear. It just appears that way. Pushing your fear away, unconsciously or consciously, is what happens when you are overwhelmed. However, today you aspire to meet your fear with curiosity and with greater presence in order to transform it into something of real value.

From a human perspective, you could say that you have lived a provisional existence as a result of having autism and mental health problems. Yet your curiosity has always inspired you to remain open and see things from a different perspective. From your soul's point of view, every depression, humiliation and heartbreak has become grist for the mill; a catalyst for dropping deeper beyond the surface and superficialities of life.

Curiosity creates an openness to unfamiliar experiences, and it is often only when you are open and deeply present to the intimacy of a moment, that you can see beyond your finite perception of it. What was previously hidden can then reveal itself. This point is wonderfully brought home by the field biologist George Schaller, when somebody asked him how it was possible for him to get to know so intimately the gorillas in their natural habitat. His answer was very simple and direct: "I didn't carry a gun." Although Schaller didn't use the word "curiosity", in this context, his whole philosophy and approach in studying the gorillas' tribal structure, family life and mating behaviours, all stemmed from his undefended approach and enthusiastic spirit of enquiry. His curiosity was clearly greater than his fear.

So easy it is to adopt a defensive approach to life, especially when you have suffered so much at the hands of others' indifference and neglect. However, when curiosity becomes stronger than fear in your life, everything changes, even the concept you hold of yourself.

Your time-bound wounds, with all their thoughts, feelings and beliefs, still cause you to contract, and at times wince, but the whole drama no longer defines who you really are. This is important to acknowledge, because the extent to which you can hold tenderly your fears becomes the extent to which you will ultimately be free of them.

"The great affair, the love affair with life," says the writer Diane Ackerman, "is to live as variously as possible, to groom one's curiosity like a high-spirited thoroughbred..." You could not agree more.

23

The sacrament of tenderness

(In memory of Jean Vanier)

You who know, and whose vast knowing
is born of poverty, abundance of poverty —

make it so the poor are no longer
despised and thrown away.

Over a quarter of a century ago your life was changed forever. You heard a talk by the founder of L'Arche, Jean Vanier, in St Martin's in the fields, London. There was something about his quality of presence, combined with his Christ-like message of love for the broken and vulnerable in society, that touched your soul so deeply.

The title of the talk that life-changing day was, *From Brokenness to Wholeness,* and what you recall so vividly from the talk he gave that day was how frequently he used the word "tenderness". You went on to read many of his books, you visited L'Arche communities, and once joined him in re-enacting Jesus washing the disciples' feet, a gesture of humility and service, performed regularly in L'Arche communities throughout the world.

So much of your life you have attempted to make yourself invulnerable. So wounded you were from the pain of your past and so ashamed of your autism that you retreated into yourself. Jean Vanier touched on this in the foreword he wrote for your little book *A Painful Gift.* Eventually, life's events, together with the passing of time, drew you ever deeper into the heart of Jean Vanier's message of love; tenderly embracing *your* disability and with it all the shame and brokenness that had shaped so much of your life.

However, the greater the light, the greater the shadow. As you write these words, posthumous revelations about Jean Vanier's abuse of power and sexual impropriety towards those who came to him for support have come to light. These revelations are shocking and deeply upsetting.

All this has echoes for you in your own experience of being sexually abused as an adolescent by a doctor whose care you were in at the time. For years you suffered in silence, oscillating between spiritual flight and numbness.

Then came the time when anger pierced the veil of shame, and overwhelming loss and grief flowed through you like a tidal wave, breaching all the defences around your bruised and battered heart. You sat in the fire not knowing if you were to be tortured for eternity or transfigured. But here, in the depths of your heart, you found forgiveness. Travelling far into the darkness you found a light, and in this light and through this light you were to reconcile seemingly irreconcilable parts of your psyche. It just all happened.

Forgiveness is for you a sacrament of tenderness; a radical softening of what was previously hard within; a walking free of the prison of hurt that previously held you captive.

Jean Vanier will always have a special place in your heart. Whilst you unequivocally condemn his sexual abuse of women, it can never take away all the beauty and love he put into the world.

24

Until it takes

*I yearn to belong to something, to be contained
in an all-embracing mind that sees me
as a single thing.*

As you write these words it is thirty years ago to the day that the Berlin Wall came down.

Tears of joy rolled down your face that day as you watched the wall come tumbling down, and with it the fearful and corrupt regime that built it.

Walls have always held a deep fascination for you. As a child with autism, it always seemed that there were walls between yourself and the world. You experienced the world as dangerous and unpredictable. Eye contact, sounds, colours, spontaneous movements and gestures would often leave you feeling overwhelmed and distressed. Walls made sense to you as they protected you and made you feel safe.

Then, of course, there were the walls you built around your heart to hide away your vulnerability, shame and loneliness. Such invisible walls were harder to see and harder still to dismantle. It took enormous skill and inner strength to scale such hidden walls and to deeply understand how and why they came into being. Perhaps overcoming these barriers was one of your greatest achievements, but greater still was the courage it took to integrate yourself within this very overwhelming and complex world.

The Indian poet Rabindranath Tagore highlights this beautifully in his poem Dungeon:

I am ever busy building this wall all around; and as this wall goes up into the sky day by day I lose sight of my true being in its dark shadow.

I take pride in this great wall, and I plaster it with dust and sand lest a least hole should be left in this name;
and for all the care I take I lose sight of my true being.

The quest for this true being has taken you far and wide. It only really began when you realised that the risk of staying hidden behind your walls was far, far greater than the risk of being seen. This was by no means an overnight awakening, but slowly and in small incremental steps your life changed from this moment on.

As you reflect on the thirtieth anniversary of the Berlin Wall coming down, and after reading many accounts of those whose lives were affected by the wall, you can see many parallels with your own experience, including the very long and arduous re-unification process.

One of the interesting things about the fall of the Berlin Wall was that no one woke up that day anticipating its collapse. It simply happened. Such is the very nature of change and transformation. It simply takes what it takes... until it takes.

Part Three

Intensified sky

25

Intensified sky

The inner — what is it?
if not the intensified sky,
hurled through with birds and deep
with the winds of homecoming.

You are a spiritual being on a human journey of which autism is an integral part.

Born into a world of inescapable sensory overload, mocked and humiliated for your idiosyncratic and unusual ways of being, you withdrew into a silent world. From out of this silence came an intense longing, a longing not only to be seen, but also to see, feel and touch the world. The world within you. The world around you. You ached to be in the world, yet not to be overcome by it.

Your formal diagnosis with autism as an adult was not a distressing experience, for it was not until you could call your neurological difference by its rightful name, that you could live creatively within its limitations and abundantly through its gifts. Into this context your diagnosis was not so much about being given a label, but instead it was a moment of enlightenment whereby the full extent of your human struggle was revealed and your dignity as a human being was restored. Your inner landscape might not have changed, but the way you were now able to relate to it was changed forever.

Even though your diagnosis was a life-defining moment, there was something far greater that was set in motion that day when you discovered you had autism. You discovered that the person you believed yourself to be was a near-complete illusion. This over-identification with your adaptive self, this part of you that was so ingeniously crafted unconsciously within you in times of unbearable distress, just dissipated like the mist at the dawn of a new day. Your imperfections were still so abundantly evident, but no longer were you over-identified nor defined by them.

Such tenderness was born in this time. Your moment of enlightenment that came through your diagnosis not only revealed to you the missing piece of the jigsaw of your human journey, but it inadvertently revealed an infinitely more expansive sense of self from which your story hung.

There have been many homecomings in your life, those sublime moments when seemingly from out of nowhere a deep truth has been revealed to you. Such homecomings cannot so much be achieved, but arrived at. They most certainly cannot be programmed nor their arrival foreseen.

26

Walking in the Light

And when the day with drowsy gesture bends
And sinks to sleep beneath the evening skies,
As from each roof a tower of smoke ascends —
So does Thy Realm, my God, around me rise.

Walking is such a beautiful way of being present to yourself, others and the world around you. It also helps you relax and discharge the trapped energy in your body.

As a kinesthetic thinker, you naturally move around in order to process information and think creatively. It would be impossible for you to write and sit still without you having a complete sensory overload and meltdown. You write, therefore you move.

Rilke, like yourself, was a loner and wanderer and, like Dickens before him, would spend many hours a day meandering around the city, seeking inspiration. Often you think of them both on your urban rambles.

The rhythm of walking is not just calming for your nervous system, it is also a soothing balm for your soul. The early Quakers talked a lot about "Waiting in the Light" and even "Walking in the Light". The inner Light being a metaphor for that of God in the human soul. Quakers are called to kindle this inner Light and carry it into the world.

So easy it is in our media-driven world, to be disconnected from the body and the natural world. But walking offers you a way of reconnecting with yourself and the wisdom of God in creation. Walking for you is a spiritual practice, be it in urban or countryside locations. Often you walk not because you have somewhere to go, but simply for the joy of walking itself; a practice of exploration without destination. Your intention is to simply give your whole, undivided attention to the sensory experience of what is immediately in front of you. This helps create a space for grace to move more freely within you.

Many Quakers today talk about holding one another in the Light and it comes naturally for you to do this. But it comes even more naturally to you to *walk* with them in the Light. Just like that Light-filled encounter with Jesus and the disciples walking together on the road to Emmaus.

27

A graceful elegance

There is no image I could invent
that your presence would not eclipse.

As a spiritual director in a central London church, you learned the art of waiting; waiting quietly and unobtrusively for anyone who wished to engage with you in matters of the heart.

When you were not actively engaged in listening to people, you would often sit silently in the church. The church was a haven for many homeless people, as well as for refugees who worked in the restaurants and shops of nearby Chinatown. In quiet moments you prayed the Jesus Prayer silently to yourself; the effortless movement of your breath, mingling with the frankincense still lingering in the air from the early morning mass. In times such as this everything seemed inseparably connected to a hidden wholeness. This was epitomised by the lighting of the candles that surrounded you in the church; each candle that had been lit was lit from the silent prayers of others.

In all the years you devoted your time there, nothing touched you so deeply as seeing people sitting quietly and reverently in stillness and silence. Such graceful elegance always left you feeling so deeply alive and attuned to the world, with all its suffering and joy:

"There's room for you in the world," said Etty Hillesum, "because you know how to go inside." How these words rang true for you here, inside this place of sanctuary and refuge in the heart of London.

Silence is for you a graceful elegance, not because it can help you to hear yourself think, but because it can enable you to move beyond thought itself. In such silence you can be completely yourself, whilst at the same time completely beyond yourself. It is here in such silence your soul can at long last feel a sense of being at home in this world.

"If the beauty of kindness were to become attractive," said John O'Donohue, "it would gradually create an atmosphere of compassion which would help the weak and wounded to transfigure their lives." How deeply these words of John O'Donohue speak to you and how beautifully this brings alive the true meaning behind your role of spiritual director in this lovely little church.

28

A most tender knowing

The anguish and yearning of all those before him
became in his hands raw matter
for him to compress into one great work.

What does it really mean to be a wounded healer?

At times you feel more *wounded* than healer. Yet when you stop and deeply reflect on your life, you can see that you truly are a wounded healer, albeit a very imperfect one.

Whilst you do not define yourself by your woundedness, it has been through embracing your wounds that you have been integrated into an infinitely larger mystery, far greater than that of your own suffering.

Your disability, your struggles with anxiety and depression and all your imperfections are no longer a source of shame and embarrassment, but instead have become a source of healing for yourself and others. Through your writing, teaching of the Alexander Technique and your work as a spiritual guide, you help people help themselves to see their own struggles as an opening and an opportunity to drop deeper into the truth of who they really are.

"The world is the closed door," says Simone Weil. "It is a barrier. And at the same time it is the way through.... Every separation is a link." The same is true for your suffering. So easy it is to live a defended life around your brokenness, yet sooner or later you come to see that this is the path to an unlived life.

"The wound is the place where the Light enters you," says Rumi, but to be a wounded healer you have to deeply integrate this wound in order for the light to truly shine forth.

For you there is no greater example of a fully-integrated being and wounded healer than Jesus. Not because he died for your sins, but because of how he lived his life. Seen in this context the Gospels become a mirror and metaphor for change and transformation in your heart. Jesus not only declared that He and the Father were one, his life was lived in complete devotion and faithfulness to this deeply held conviction that he felt in his heart.

There are times in life when you feel you have truly failed and that your woundedness has concealed rather than revealed anything of value. Yet the fact remains that you have the capacity to understand the human condition, not in spite of your losses and imperfections but because of them. From out of this deep understanding comes a most tender knowing, and it is through such a knowing that you touch the world.

29

Writing as a way of being

Like words that in the silence clearer grow
As they unfold before thy will to know...

You write, not so much to understand yourself, but to move beyond yourself. And whilst you are not what you write, it is often through the very act of writing that who you really are is revealed.

"Find out the reason that commands you to write"; said Rilke, "see whether it has spread its roots into the very depth of your heart..." Wise words indeed. And you learned that to write at depth, you have to get out of the way of your *internal censor*. Whilst this logical part of your mind might serve you well in other aspects of your writing career, such as communicating with your publisher and giving promotional talks, when it comes to writing about the inner life, your internal censor will often be your greatest of enemies.

You write for the joy of writing itself. Your main concern is not if your writing may be received well or not, nor do you give credence to the critical voices within you that can often say you are wasting your time or that your writing is not good enough. Such dissenting voices may be nothing short of sabotage. A classic example would be Vincent Van Gogh, who had a wonderful way of responding to these unhelpful voices within; he simply painted in sheer defiance of them, with a result which was little short of miraculous. As for doubts, you often reflect on the advice Rilke gave to the young Franz Xaver Kappus, immortalised in *Letters to a Young Poet*: "When doubts arise, simply 'school them': instead of being demolishers they will be among your best workers."

In channelling your thoughts in a more mindful direction, you often ask yourself the question "What's happening right here, right now, within you?" Such a question, asked with an open heart and an inquiring mind, helps in "pinching" you awake from out of the slumber of your habitual thinking and into the present moment. By no longer resisting your experience, you are allowing what is moving within you to simply *be* moving within you. By doing this, you are free to distill the very essence that you wish to bring out in your writing. This is what you call writing as a way of being.

Writing in this contemplative way creates within you something akin to a nervous system, a web of connectivity, helping you to connect with previously disconnected feelings, memories and sensations. However, writing as a way of being is so much more than reclaiming your feelings and your own search for private meaning. It is writing from this deep place within that connects you with the deepest part of your humanity—your heart; that place which remains after biology and psychology have attempted to define you.

Writing as a way of being moves you beyond the surface and into the depths of your being. Slowly, ever so slowly, you become less interested in your thoughts, feelings, memories and sensations, and more interested in the One that is aware of them. Your deeper Self.

30

Heart-Work

Enfold you with my heart as with a hand.
Hold my heart, my brain will take fire of you...

Often you ask yourself, is there an image that conveys what is moving within you, right here, right now?

Such a question is most useful to ask yourself when you feel stuck or in some way resisting something that is causing you to suffer. So when you have found an image that resonates with you, allow it to drop into that infinitely expansive space within. Your heart. Then, just wait. The waiting is crucial. The temptation is always to try and work your problems out with your head.

Whilst you may have some success in resolving some day-to-day concerns through your intellect, the deeper questions will often require a very different approach. As Rilke explains in *Letters to a Young Poet,* logic can only take you so far: "I beg you, to have patience with everything unresolved in your heart and to try to love the questions themselves as if they were locked rooms or books written in a very foreign language." Then he adds, "Don't search for the answers, which could not be given to you now, because you would not be able to live them. And the point is to live everything. Live the questions now. Perhaps then, someday far in the future, you will gradually, without even noticing it, live your way into the answer."

And for you, answers often come when you least expect them. Often it is through surrendering into Silence and allowing its wisdom to permeate your whole being that brings about a transformation of heart and mind.

Your thinking mind will almost always think it knows what is best, yet there is an inner knowing within you and your work is to simply get out of the way of this inner knowing.

31

Being love

But everything that touches you and me
Welds us as played strings sound one melody.
Where is the instrument whence the sounds flow?
And whose the master-hand that holds the bow?
O! Sweet song —

You fell in love with her the very first time you saw her face. There was no uncertainty, and in that moment, you held within yourself both an ending and a beginning.

Slowly, ever so slowly, who you really are to each other unfolds. Yet it is not so much what you have together, but knowing who you really are within that togetherness that is the deeper measure. Here the words of Rilke speak to you: "Love consists in this, that two solitudes protect and touch and greet each other."

In such solitude you are in solidarity with your true nature. It is here that there is no separation, only connection; the experience of being one, within the necessary appearance of being two. You cannot transform what you have not first blessed with presence, and love flows from out of the receptivity of this presence. Take time to listen deeply to yourself, to your beloved, to each other, for what you give your attention to, you give reality to.

It may be true to say that you do not know what you have until you lose it. However, it is equally true to say that you will never really know the fullness of your losses in life until you have held tenderly in your hands all that you have ever wanted. It is here that your beloved opens up within you a doorway into and beyond your brokenness.

Allowing yourself to be vulnerable with your beloved deepens trust and closeness. This can feel like a great risk to take, but the greater risk is to give in to fear and make yourself invulnerable, for this will only distance you from the love that is your deepest longing. Such a love evokes in you the innate love that has always been in you; the love you are sees its own radiance in your beloved.

"Conscious love," says modern-day mystic and Episcopal priest Cynthia Bourgeault, "is love in the service of inner transformation—or, if you prefer, inner transformation in the service of love." And it is this very "inner transformation in the service of love" that makes your relationship with your beloved so vibrantly alive and so deeply meaningful.

32

An exquisite risk

I circle around God, around the primordial tower.
I've been circling for thousands of years
and I still don't know: am I a falcon,
a storm, or a great song?

Something greater than you, is working through you.

Shaping your entire life around this "something greater" is without doubt an exquisite risk. For there is much you have to lose in giving your life over to this power greater than yourself, none more so than the concept you hold of yourself. For who you *really* are, is not who you think you are.

"We live, to some extent, as an imaginary character in an imagined world," says psychotherapist and author Judith Blackstone. "Whether this fantasy is a romance or a horror story, it is not as satisfying as the direct experience of life." Judith Blackstone's statement deeply resonates with you. Your deeper identification is as a Soul, rather than as a writer, father or person on the autism spectrum. However, embracing tenderly all these things is an integral part of your spiritual journey.

You live life courageously and skillfully. Too much rigidity and control, and you close yourself off to the life of the spirit. Too much flexibility and tolerance, and you open yourself to overwhelm and meltdown. Some days you miss the mark and get it all wrong. You fail to communicate with those you love and end up hurting them. Some days you are unable to take the risk of opening to life, you clamp down, get angry, feel hurt and retreat into yourself. Your inner light becomes obscured.

The poet Mark Nepo captures this challenge to live a more light-filled and tender life in his beautiful book *The Book of Awakening*:

> *We waste so much energy trying to cover up who we are, when beneath every attitude is the want to be loved, and beneath every anger is a wound to be healed, and beneath every sadness is the fear that there will not be enough time.*

> *When we hesitate in being direct, we unknowingly slip something on, some added layer of protection that keeps us from feeling the world, and often that thin covering is the beginning of a loneliness which, if not put down, diminishes our chances for joy.*

> *It's like wearing gloves every time we touch something, and then, forgetting we chose to put them on, we complain that nothing feels quite real. In this way, our challenge each day is not to get dressed to face the world, but to unglove ourselves...*

And it is this very "un-gloving" and allowing yourself to be seen that is ultimately the most exquisite risk of all.

33

Farewell

For we are only the rind and the leaf.

The great death, that each of us carries inside,
is the fruit.

The last years of your adoptive father's life were harrowing and deeply upsetting. Yet a closeness was born in this time that evaded you both throughout your entire lives.

Your father grew up close to poverty and in the shadow of two devastating world wars, the consequences of which left deep emotional scars. Coming from such a deprived and wounding background made his entry into medical school and his eventual qualification as a doctor even more remarkable.

Your father was a man driven to success by the indignity and suffering of his past, yet with each success brought its very own failure. Unable to relax, he turned to alcohol and tranquilizers to soften the hard and jagged edges of his mind. Yet his deeply-rooted feelings of insecurity and inadequacy drove him on relentlessly.

Unexpressed grief was the elephant in the room that seemed to fill the whole house and permeate your entire childhood. The great war effort had not abated and daily life was like living on the front line of a war zone; each member of the family anxiously holding their own perilously-held position.

Your position was clearly one of family scapegoat. Having autism and appearing so different, there was a certain inevitability about all this. Your family was so driven to distraction by their unrelenting need to keep at a distance their overwhelming feelings of grief and loss. This gave birth to the overwhelming need for control and projection.

Being labelled the "mad" one made everyone else look sane, or at the very least beyond reproach.

It was into this merciless and unrelentingly cruel environment that you lived out your childhood. Daily you were mocked and humiliated by your father for the way you looked and spoke, and for all your idiosyncratic ways and mannerisms that were an integral part of your being.

Much of your life since has been spent healing from your childhood experiences and the enormous weight of being the family scapegoat. You have journeyed through denial, outrage, depression, grief, and arrived at forgiveness. Such forgiveness is not a one-shot deal, but instead a continuous unfolding from the hurt that previously held you captive.

Towards the end of your father's life he suffered a series of strokes that left him bed bound, paralysed and utterly dependent on others. Now he was totally powerless over everything and everyone. These last ten years of his life were extremely painful to witness, yet something of enormous value was found in this time. His suffering not only broke him down, it also broke him open.

In these last days of your father's life, it was as though he became a child again and met the child within you. Here you met each other as if for the first time. At last there were no distractions. Now there was nowhere to go and nothing to do, just two souls looking at each other, forgiving each other and saying... farewell.

34

The Serenity Prayer

I thank you, deep power
that works me ever more lightly
in ways I can't make out.

The Serenity Prayer, adopted by Alcoholics Anonymous and its affiliated twelve-step programmes, has been one of the greatest comforts in your life.

Whilst the Jesus Prayer helps you become sensitive to God at all times, as well as offering you an anchor point, the Serenity Prayer helps you when everything appears to have fallen apart, and when everything feels completely hopeless. It is as though the very saying of the prayer opens up a space within your fearful heart through which you can then more easily accept your powerlessness:

God grant me the serenity
to accept the things I cannot change,
the courage to change the things I can,
and the wisdom to know the difference.

"I pray," said C.S. Lewis, "because I can't help myself. I pray because I'm helpless. I pray because the need flows out of me all the time, waking and sleeping. It doesn't change God. It changes me." This beautiful statement from C.S. Lewis speaks volumes to you about the power of prayer, and particularly the Serenity Prayer.

The great power of the Serenity Prayer comes not from the choice of words, but instead what the words evoke in you, especially when you feel distressed and overwhelmed. The effectiveness of prayer does not depend on the intensity with which you pray, but on the depth of openness and humility which you bring to the prayer.

In essence, saying the Serenity Prayer helps you get out of the way of yourself, that small contracted sense of who you think yourself to be and enables you to be held in God's loving embrace. It is all about letting go of control and handing it all over to God. The more you let go the more peace you feel. Thai Buddhist monk Ajahn Chah says it so well:

> If you let go a little, you will have a little peace.
> If you let go a lot, you will have a lot of peace.
> If you let go completely, you will have complete peace.

Quietly practising the Serenity Prayer over many years, you have come to understand its depth and enormous value. You have come to see why serenity and peacefulness of mind are so important in the spiritual life. And even though you still often find the world a distressing and overwhelming place to be in, you have your place of refuge in such a beautiful humble little prayer.

35

I love you, gentlest of Ways

I love you, gentlest of Ways
who ripened us as we wrestled with you.

The Quaker Way of being is so deeply attuned to your personality and soul alike.

In many ways you have always been a natural Quaker. The longing for silence and a spirituality that is inseparably interwoven with the testimonies of Peace, Equality, Truth, Simplicity and Sustainability, make the Quakers a most natural home for you. These values and testimonies are not relegated to the margins, nor forced into little societies or groups, but instead are the living, beating heart of the community. This integration creates an environment of wholeness, strength and vitality. And in so doing it affirms in a very clear and coherent way exactly what Quakers are and what we hold dear.

Of all the religious and spiritual communities you have experienced, the Quakers have offered you a home like no other. There are many reasons for this, but one that stands out above all else is the radical acceptance of difference. Whether this difference is one's sexuality, a difference of opinion or view, or a different way of perceiving and experiencing God.

"Our life is love," said Isaac Penington, "and peace, and tenderness; and bearing one with another, and forgiving one another, and not laying accusations one against another; but praying one for another, and helping one another up with a tender hand." This statement by Isaac Penington, one of the early members of the Religious Society of Friends, speaks to you. For it embodies not only the essence of Jesus' teachings but also the spirit out of which the Quakers came into being and have sustained their radical vision for well over three and a half centuries.

You remember the day you first stepped into a Quaker meeting. It was as though you had come in from a lifetime of being in the cold, the coldness of not being truly and deeply accepted as a Soul and as a human being.

36

A beautiful practice

... you Limitless Now.

Like many Quakers you have a deep respect for other spiritual paths, practices and teachers. None more so than the Zen Buddhist master Thich Nhat Hanh, affectionately known to us as Thay.

Thay and his Community of Interbeing, have played such an important part in your life. Through this disciplined, mindful practice you have not only acquired the ability to be more present in life, but also learned how to transform your suffering into something of deep and lasting value. The Quaker way and Thay's way have together woven a tapestry of kindness and presence into your life.

"Our mind is like a field," says Thich Nhat Hanh, "where every kind of seed is planted—seeds of suffering, anger, happiness, and peace. The quality of our life depends on the quality of the seeds in our mind. If we know how to water seeds of joy and transform seeds of suffering, then understanding, love and compassion will flower."

Living with autism and complex post-traumatic stress disorder, there are many unwholesome seeds in you. Such seeds have caused you to suffer enormously throughout your life. Seeds such as: phobia, obsessive-compulsive disorder, depression and anxiety. You have throughout your life diligently taken these seeds, these painful experiences, to psychotherapists, psychologists, healers and the many recovery fellowships available today. As a result, you have been able to move forward in your life. However, so easy it is to unknowingly water such unwholesome seeds. You do this by being either inattentive or giving undue attention to your seeds.

Much of your early life was spent running away from your suffering. Then came the time when running away was no longer possible. Your suffering caught up with you. However, you did not have the necessary skills then in order to welcome and deeply befriend these terrified and overwhelmed elements within you.

Thay and his Community of Interbeing have given you the tools to *be* with yourself and in so doing live a more embodied, joyful and integrated life. Mindfulness is for you the cultivating of Soul consciousness and, as such, it occupies centre-stage in your life. A life that was once overwhelmed with sorrow and despair has become fertile ground out of which flowers of peace and joy can grow.

37

The Way of a Pilgrim

You, the great homesickness we could never shake off,
you, the forest that always surrounded us...

The Way of a Pilgrim is one of your favourite books. In so many ways the main character's wandering existence, alongside his deep desire to live a life of unceasing prayer, has many parallels in your own life.

In the very opening chapter of *The Way of a Pilgrim*, the pilgrim lets us into his heart:

> *I heard many very good sermons on prayer, but all of them gave directions on prayer in general: what prayer is; the necessity of prayer; what the fruits of prayer are; but how to achieve such prayer? No one talked about that. There was one sermon about prayer in the spirit and unceasing prayer, but nothing on how to attain it.*

What follows is the most beautiful story of how the pilgrim journeys through mid-nineteenth-century southern and central Ukraine, Russia and Siberia. His deep longing takes him to many teachers who help him in practising the Jesus Prayer as a way and means of achieving his primary intention of intimacy with God at all times.

You recall such a life-defining moment in your life when you were a young man. You were in the audience listening to a well-known mystic and contemplative. After an hour or so of talking about the spiritual life the monk requested that everyone share a time of silence together. What immediately followed was a quiet riot of activity as the vast majority of people in the audience awkwardly shuffled and re-organised themselves into their "postures of being". This was a moment of epiphany for you. You observed that night, and on numerous other occasions in such contemplative settings in the years to come, how the vast majority of people present were just not conscious of this disparity. And even if this was brought to their attention, they would likely, as was the case with the pilgrim in the opening chapter, be clueless as to how to address this lack of integration.

Like the pilgrim, what interested you above all was how you could weave this *way of being* into a seamless garment that you could live and breathe out into the world. Such a quest has taken you far and wide and, like the pilgrim, you have met many wise guides who have patiently instructed you on prayer of the heart and the integration of mind, body and soul.

The joy has been, and continues to be, in the journey. A journey so blunderingly undertaken, yet through patience and perseverance, a deeper love continues to grow within you.

Part Four

Homecoming

38

The Winds of Homecoming

hurled through with birds and deep
with the winds of homecoming.

The person you think yourself to be is subject to all that life has thrown at it. Yet the truth of who you really are, your soul, is beyond personal happiness and unhappiness.

At times, thoughts such as: "How can I, so broken, so vulnerable, be of any value in this life?" plague and torment you. Such painful and disqualifying thoughts have deeply wounded you in the past. Yet the truth is your very brokenness, your vulnerability itself, gives you eyes to truly see the world, and a heart to deeply feel it.

The wound may well be the place where the light enters you, but it is also the place where darkness can enter too. Your earliest experiences of being mocked and daily humiliated for being different weighed heavily on your soul. And your experience of mental collapse and subsequent hospitalisation as a young man disturbed and haunted you for years. The American author Anne Morrow Lindbergh speaks deeply to you when she says:

> *I do not believe that sheer suffering teaches. If suffering alone taught, all the world would be wise, since everyone suffers. To suffering must be added mourning, understanding, patience, love, openness and the willingness to remain vulnerable.*

This "openness and the willingness to remain vulnerable" is crucial if you wish to be intimate with life.

Your true freedom lies in discovering that which is ever present regardless of all that comes your way in life. Your wounds may well be the place where the Light enters you, but you are so much more than your wounds. You are the Light that shines through them.

There is the thinking about life and then there is the entering into it. Your entry point has always been your brokenness and your vulnerability. When you understand this, not just intellectually, but in the bones of your being, the Winds of Homecoming will guide you home.

39

A God hidden in Tenderness

My body glows in every vein and blooms
To fullest flower since I first knew thee,
My walk unconscious pride and power assumes;
Who art thou then — thou who awaitest me?

The washing of the disciples' feet is for you one of the most moving stories in the Gospels.
Touch brings presence home. As a teacher of the Alexander Technique you see the transformation that is set in motion through the power of touch and presence. To be touched with love and tenderness can change one's life in a most extraordinary way.

You often reflect on Jesus washing the disciples' feet. Putting yourself right into the centre of the drama and imagining what you might feel. More often than not you can relate to Simon Peter's reaction and feel completely overcome with awkwardness, even at the thought of someone just touching you with such intimacy. So much easier is it to hide behind your role of being the giver, than to receive and be touched by another.

When Simon Peter refuses to let Jesus wash his feet, Jesus' response is truly astonishing:

Unless I wash you, you have no part with me.

It is as though Jesus is saying, "If you want to follow me, you must learn to bear the pain that tenderness will bring forth in you."

The taking off of one's sandals is a movement towards intimacy, "in-to-me-you-see". But nothing can really prepare one for the experience of truly being touched and seen by God. All the miracles in the Gospels pale into insignificance compared to being seen and touched at such depth by the living God.

How overwhelmingly difficult it must have been for the disciples to truly understand the inner meaning behind this experience, let alone integrate it into their lives. You feel for each and every one of them as they desperately attempt to grasp the magnitude of Jesus' teaching.

"... you should do as I have done to you." These words said by Jesus after he washed the disciples' feet, make it clear that the central message of his teaching is to be of service to the world. To *be love* in the world.

The message is clear, that real change and power comes not from the "top down", but from the "bottom up". In Jesus' kingdom the world is turned upside down and inside out. Leaders become servants and Jesus becomes such a servant. A God hidden in Tenderness.

40

A twilight dwelling

Then suddenly you're left all alone
with your body that can't love you
and your will that can't save you.

Today you received your cancer diagnosis. Yet even before you were to hear those fate-filled words: "I'm very sorry to have to tell you...", you had already joined all the dots and read between the lines. You knew.

Almost immediately that wise saying by Allen Saunders came to mind: "Life is what happens to us while we are making other plans." Now, the only plans you were able to entertain were how you were to prepare your mind and body for either the radioactive assault that was coming its way or the loss of an organ.

Yet the most difficult part of the drama was the waiting, the not knowing. Your fear was not so much around disease, dying or even death itself, but instead the prospect of all those endless hospital appointments; the system's conveyor belt of cancer care. Suspended between two worlds, the world where plans are made and the world where long-term plans no longer really feature.

In quieter moments, when you were able to still your mind, an interior silence was found which eventually opened to an inner spaciousness. Tenderly, ever so tenderly, you placed your hand on your chest and named the entire drama of thoughts, feelings and emotions racing through your awareness: fear of how your beloved partner would cope, powerlessness, fear of incapacity, anger, irritation, depression, anxiety, shame, confusion, disorientation, disorganisation, loss of appetite, chronic tiredness, suicidal thoughts... the list could have gone on and on and on.

As you write these words a whole week has passed. A week in which you have continued to lovingly witness and hold tenderly the entire drama spinning itself out within your psyche. As the controller in you releases, you open to a deeper vulnerability, and yet there remains a place within you where even fear cannot touch; a place where grace moves unimpeded, and peace can be found.

On a certain level, having cancer could be seen as something you would want to avoid and wish away. But on a deeper level, you simply see your disease as just part of the work that you're here to do.

Your body is a twilight dwelling, a temporary abode, the place where you meet and touch the world.

41

Unlearning your way back to God

Even when we don't desire it,
God is ripening.

Unlearning for you is not so much about forgetting or discarding. Nor is it about superimposing the new on top of the old. Unlearning for you is all about how tenderly you can witness and hold yourself in the world. For the extent to which you can practise this and engage with the world from out of this tender place, will be the extent to which you can create new pathways and a deeper connection with yourself and God.

As a teacher of the Alexander Technique, you help people to help themselves to be more present in their lives. The body thus becomes a vehicle for change and transformation, offering a new way of perceiving oneself and the world.

Through your presence, sense of humour and the gentle use of your hands, a new way of being is revealed to the pupil. Mindful awareness of these principles in your own life has enabled you to weave your inner and outer life together in a much more coherent way.

Your experience of the Alexander Technique, as a pupil and as a teacher for the last quarter of a century, has led you to believe that its "means whereby" approach offers a very practical and pragmatic way of living a more embodied life. This creates a bridge between contemplative practice and the compelling drama of the world. As a result, this way of being, that you call *being en route*, becomes a most natural foundation for spiritual practice.

The experience of training to be an Alexander Technique teacher drew you ever deeper into the mystical and contemplative paths of all the world's great religions. What you sought then as a young man was not so much information, but transformation, and not so much religion, but relationship. Relationship *with* God.

Through Alexander work you came to experience the great power that comes from releasing into integrity, the integrity not just of the head, neck and back, but an integrity of one's whole being. An Integrity that came about not by learning anything, but by *un*learning *every*thing.

42

That which is wide and timeless

Then the knowing comes: I can open
to another life that's wide and timeless.

Your challenge in this life is to affirm your human struggle within the context of that which is eternal. Your soul. This place that Rilke describes as being "wide and timeless".

Writing about this "life that's wide and timeless" is no easy undertaking, for your experiences lose their vitality long before you have attempted to translate them into words. You may well be an author, but words cannot "author" an experience. Perhaps this is what the great philosopher and theologian Saint Thomas Aquinas meant when, shortly before his death, he famously said:

The end of my labours has come. All that I have written appears to be as so much straw after the things that have been revealed to me.

These words of Aquinas are always in the forefront of your mind each and every time you set out to communicate and write about the inner life. You live within two dimensions, two levels of reality that are simultaneously playing themselves out. On the human level suffering is seen as a hindrance and something to be avoided, at times, at all cost. Whilst from a soul's perspective, suffering can be seen as grace. The challenge you face is not so much how you adequately communicate this in words, but how you live this mystery out in your life. This is beautifully conveyed for you in Rilke's poem "The Life Being Lived":

And yet, though we strain
against the deadening grip
of daily necessity,
I sense there is this mystery:

All life is being lived.

Who is living it, then?
Is it the things themselves,
or something waiting inside them,
like an unplayed melody in a flute?

Is it the winds blowing over the waters?
Is it the branches that signal to each other?

Is it flowers
interweaving their fragrances,
or streets, as they wind through time?

Is it the animals, warmly moving,
or the birds, that suddenly rise up?

Who lives it, then? God, are you the one
who is living life?

43

Solitude as a way of being

Solitude is like a rain
That from the sea at dusk begins to rise;
It floats remote across the far-off plain
Upward into its dwelling-place, the skies,
Then o'er the town it slowly sinks again.

So much of spiritual life is about letting go. Letting go of the illusions you hold of yourself, others and the world.

You have always had an insatiable desire for truth. A longing to see things as they really are, not merely as they appear to be. This quest for truth started early in life and possibly had its roots in the experience of growing up unhappily in your adopted home. Perhaps it was this overwhelming sense of being "dis-placed" that became the catalyst for you to deeply question who you really were and where you *really* belonged.

As a result, you were forever seeking out a refuge away from the endless misery of family life, a place where you could be safe and come home to yourself. In many ways you lost so much. Yet one thing you never lost was your enquiring nature and your unrelenting drive to understand yourself and the world around you.

Today you are no longer driven to solitude, you are drawn into it. Whilst memories of loss and loneliness often come into your awareness in the silence of solitude, you have learned how to *be* with such feelings in a way that does not unbalance you. In such solitude you can find your true home, a space within you that reaches out to life, in contrast to the loneliness of your past where you painfully retreated into yourself.

"We are not human beings having a spiritual experience," said the Jesuit, Pierre Teilhard de Chardin. "We are spiritual beings having a human experience." In other words, your true identity is that of God and your challenge is to affirm this deeper reality within the drama of being human.

Solitude for you today is not so much about withdrawing from the world, but a way of *being* in it and not being overcome by it. A way of being fully present to yourself and of being in solidarity with your true and timeless nature.

44

"Be" the mystery at the crossroads

What mystery breaks over me now?
In its shadow I come into life.
For the first time I am alone with you —

You are both the infinite ocean and the crashing of its waves; both its surface and its depths.

When you only give your attention to the surface of life, you are only superficially awake. Yet suffering has taken you deeper, and your willingness to stay with the discomfort of your suffering whilst remaining open to its teaching, has taken you deeper still.

Today you move more gracefully between life's surfaces and its depths, to such an extent that you are able to *be* more in the world and not be so overcome by it. Relatively speaking you seem to be in control of your life; appearing to make decisions and being the creator of your own destiny. But the deeper truth is that you are not the "doer" of your actions, nor the "thinker" of your thoughts, and that the person you believe yourself to be is ultimately powerless over absolutely everything.

All of this is a deep disappointment and humiliation to your small self, who forever seeks certainty, outcomes and control. Yet time and time again the illusion of you being in control is revealed to you. Sometimes this can feel like a blessing, whilst at other times it can feel like a curse.

You write these words in a beautiful churchyard in Hampstead overlooking the City of London. Your body aches and tiredness makes your eyes heavy. You listen deeply to your body and what it is trying to communicate to you after your recent surgery to remove your cancer. The physical pain and discomfort become more bearable when you can stop resisting the uncomfortable experience and allow the experience to be just as it is.

Something greater than you is moving through you. "Be the mystery at the crossroads of your senses, the meaning discovered there," said Rilke.

Being the "mystery at the crossroads" for you means standing at the intersection where that which is fleeting and that which is eternal meet; holding both the relative and ultimate dimensions with the utmost tenderness, humour and grace.

45

What has been whispered to you

All creation holds its breath, listening within me,
because, to hear you, I keep silent.

You learnt long ago, how much you did not know.

Whilst lying motionless on an MRI scanner recently, you realised there was at least one thing you *did* know. You knew that you were so much more than this body which would soon decay and pass away. And as the cold dye injected into your veins made its way to your cancer, you saw as if never before, that there was nothing to be gained by worrying about or resisting any experience. With this awareness you simply let go and allowed the experience to be as it was.

Experience itself is for you like an ever-flowing ocean of awareness, in which you have only a sliver of choice as to whether to identify with the compelling drama of its waves, or with the silence of its depths. All this you pondered as the scanner vibrated and rattled out its merry tunes. You reflected on your life of contemplation and prayer and how this is in itself merely preparation for diving into this ocean of existence, and trusting you will be carried home by the tide of love. The same love which Pierre Teilhard de Chardin talked of, that was for him "the very physical structure of the universe".

Then, from out of the stillness deep within you an inner voice whispered to you: "You are here to learn how to hold yourself tenderly on this earth, whilst at the same time to surrender this very self completely over to God." How you live with this paradox will determine whether you will find happiness or whether happiness will evade you in this life.

Holding your fear tenderly means for you to be fully present to yourself and others and in so doing seeing your common humanity. The poet Mark Nepo touches on this when he said that there is "a kinship of gratitude that bonds us in our common experience of pain. For at the heart of every suffering, if we can find it, is God and each other."

Under the scanner that day you felt this "kinship of gratitude" towards the medical staff and fellow cancer patients. You felt it again as you were anxiously waiting with your partner in the oncologist's waiting room for the results of your tests. And as you write these words you extend this kinship of gratitude to all humanity, because deep down we are all carrying each other Home. And often in the most unforeseen and mysterious of ways.

46

Prayer of the heart

When I go toward you
it is with my whole life.

Prayer is not what you do, it is who you are: a murmuring stream of the heart that reaches out as well as within. Deeply within, to that mysterious part of you. Your deepest Self.

You pray not so much to give thanks, but instead to *be* that thankfulness; for the very act of prayer is a joy in itself. Why? Because whether you sing, chant, talk or just bow your head in silence, you pray because you have a song to sing, and prayer for you is such a song. As St Catherine of Siena herself said:

All the way to Heaven is heaven...

You have long since abandoned the attempt to understand prayer, for you cannot get your head around it; you can only get your heart around it. It has been your experience that the potency and power of prayer does not depend on the intensity with which you pray, but on the devotion and tenderness which you take to the prayer itself.

You have always aspired to live your life quietly and prayerfully, attuning yourself to what in later life you would call that which is timeless and eternal, becoming sensitive to God in all things and at all times. So when you found the Jesus Prayer as a young man your heart jumped for joy, for here was *your* means whereby your deeper desire could be actualised.

You discovered that coordinating the Jesus Prayer with your in-breath and out-breath simply helped you to sleep by offering you a soothing alternative to your restless thoughts. Then, gradually over time, the gentle repetition of this ancient devotional prayer helped you stay more centred and less distracted by the endless clamour and drama of the world. Everyday life, with all its ups and downs, gradually became infused with deeper meaning and purpose:

Jesus Christ, Son of God,
have mercy on me...

Said tenderly, quietly and with an open heart, the Jesus Prayer permeates your whole being, helping you move from your intellect into your heart. The gentle repetition of the prayer creates a space for grace to come through; taking you from the surface and into the depths of your being throughout the day. Slowly, ever so slowly, the prayer prays itself in the same way that breathing breathes itself. Prayer and "pray-er" both dissolve as a more diffuse and objectless awareness comes into being; drifting on the wordless ocean of awareness. This is what it means for you to truly rest in God.

From the very first moment you wake in the morning, to the very last moments before you sleep at night, the Jesus Prayer is your constant companion in living life more faithfully and deeply.

47

An anchored presence

I am the dream you are dreaming.
When you want to awaken, I am that wanting:
I grow strong in the beauty you behold.
And with the silence of stars I enfold...

Every fortnight you sit quietly in the Julian of Norwich Church and its adjacent cell. It is here that the fourteenth to early fifteenth-century Christian mystic and anchoress lived out her ministry in solitude and contemplation.

Six hundred years after her death, Julian's "anchored presence" is still so deeply felt here. How you love to sit in this contemplative space, watching the sun go down as the candles softly illuminate this tiny holy place. Often your mind turns to the enormous upheaval and drama that Julian would have lived through in the fourteenth and fifteenth centuries: intense violence, plague, revolts and extraordinary political and religious upheaval.

Julian was without doubt a woman of extraordinary faith, which gave her a unique vantage point in understanding the radical message of the Gospels; a beacon of light in such overwhelmingly dark times in which many sick and vulnerable people sought her counsel. Her message is as powerful today as it was then, that "all shall be well...", and that our true freedom lies in discovering the loving tenderness of Christ which is ever present regardless of ever-changing experiences.

However, silence has not always been so welcoming. For much of your early life you lived in a silent world. You became mute out of sheer terror of being mocked, humiliated and taken advantage of; the silence you lived in was not so much golden, as very dark. The transition from suffering in silence, to being found within it, was long and arduous, and in many ways you could say that you started this perilous journey many years ago within these very walls where Julian lived and gave counsel.

On the surface it may appear that you and Julian lived very different lives. Whilst this is undeniably true, there remains a deeper truth, that as a result of intense and overwhelming suffering you were both given eyes to see reality in a radically new way. For you both, this way was not so much governed by doctrinal rules and morality, but by grace, tenderness and transformation through love.

Sitting here you ponder on these things. You reflect on Julian's "shewings", and the "painful gift" that has been your own life. You close your eyes and are drawn ever deeper into the formless silence which echoes within these walls. You smile inwardly and give thanks. For everything.

48

A gathered silence

He who will overcome you
is working in silence.

In the gathered silence of a Quaker meeting for worship, you leave behind the noise and clamour of the world and enter into a very different dimension.

At times, a solemnity and depth of power pervades the silence, and a profound sense of presence fills the entire meeting. In such times the person you think yourself to be fades into the background and who you really are comes to the fore. It is from this more soulful perspective that a bigger picture emerges, and with it all your petty affairs that plague you in the world pale into insignificance. It is as though you cease to identify with the roles you play out in the world—autistic person, father, survivor, son, teacher, writer, and instead you drop deeper into the truth of who you really are; that part of you which is timeless, unchanging and eternal. Your soul.

Quakers do not have creeds, as it is felt that they can so easily limit or confine a person's perception of truth. Such creeds, formal statements and belief systems were so useful for you when you first started out on your spiritual journey. However, today your intuition tells you that you will sooner or later have to abandon them all in order to reach the "Greater Shore".
The gathered silence is but an invitation to go deeper. You cannot get there; you can only *be* there. As a result, you experience not so much a foretaste of what awaits you, but what you are in essence right here, right now. This is not so much about being

in right relationship with God, as discovering your true identity as "that of God".

Although the power of a gathered silence is always there, attuning yourself to it is quite a different matter. One of the greatest obstacles to letting go into a gathered silence is your restless and agitated mind. However, you know well that it is not your absence of afflictions that defines who you are, but instead your faithfulness within the drama of it all that is the deeper measure.

In the gathered silence of a Quaker meeting for worship, you enter into a mystery that draws you ever deeper. This is so beautifully expressed by Isaac Penington, when he famously said, "The end of words is to bring us to the knowledge of things beyond which words can utter."

49

So tender

Before us great Death stands
Our fate held close within his quiet hands.
When with proud joy we lift Life's red wine up
To drink deep of the mystic shining cup
And ecstasy through all our being leaps —
Death bows his head and weeps.

Her breathing is shallow, even and calm.

Suspended between sleep and waking states, your dear friend lies motionless in bed, dying. Her emaciated body consumed by cancer, her ribcage as delicate as a tiny sparrow. You place your hand tenderly upon her chest, hoping that your fingers will in some way become like floating ribs, supporting her desperate struggle for life, a life you know is ending before your eyes.

You sit in the silence. Waiting. Watching. Praying. The clock ticks away. You count each tick, until it drives you to distraction. You reach out for the clock, but stop in mid-movement. Perhaps your friend takes comfort in the metronome effect offered by the ticking clock? Then you realise that it is not so much the noise the clock is making that is disconcerting, but the march of time itself. Perhaps in feeling such overwhelming powerlessness you need to take control of something?... counting, counting, remembering!

Your mind wanders. You try and put dates to the many wonderful times you have shared with your dear friend. Yet whilst your head is obsessed with the details, your heart just recalls the memories. Memories scattered and sprinkled like dandelion seeds in the winds of passing time. Tears fall from your eyes as your dear, beautiful friend whispers, "I love you, so tender, so tender my love."

Here at your friend's bedside you feel that which is eternal holding you both. Eternal, not in the sense of time abundance, but in the very absence of time itself. With her last breath she looks at you with such beauty and grace as if to say that dying is perfectly safe and the most natural thing in the world.

Everywhere around you is silence... you leave your friend's lifeless body and walk out into the busy high street. Yet all you hear is silence. The silence feels overwhelming. It also feels strangely comforting, like when snow covers an entire area and everything, even sound itself, is cushioned.

You watch the sun breaking through the clouds. The first autumnal breeze blows upon your cheeks and from out of the silence you hear those tender and final words your friend whispered to you:

"I love you, so tender, so tender my love."

50

Rearranged by life

Who is it, then? God, are you the one
who is living life?

It took me three years to write this book. In this time, I lost two of my closest friends to cancer. Then, soon after their passing, I too was diagnosed with cancer. However, I also met my partner and soul mate, Helen, at this time. Now, from out of nowhere, the world is gripped by a global pandemic.

Life is what happens, when we're busy making other plans. How true this saying really is. For however much I attempt to plan and organise my life, it is often the case that it is Life and not me that does the arranging – and rearranging. When I go with this flow, this flow of life, and not work against it by trying to work everything out, everything can be seen as grace. Absolutely everything. Even a pandemic.

Life's events, together with the passing of time, will often play their part in reopening and reawakening painful experiences. This was very much the case for me with respect to living through the early stages of the Coronavirus pandemic in London, where the fear of contagion was palpable, mirrored in people's faces wherever I looked. We lived in a hyper-reality, which was echoed by the eerie surrealism of the capital's empty streets. Time took on another dimension, and the life that I had known ceased to exist.

When the lockdown restrictions were partially lifted, so too were my defences. Then the floodgates opened. It took me a while to put some space between the trauma of my past and the present. Lockdown brought out that which had been locked in and hidden away within me.

Staying open whilst being vulnerable, holding mystery and not taking flight, these things require skill. They also require grace. Creating such a space for grace is often only found in moments of quiet and solitude. Yet solitude can often feel like a lonely and uninhabited place for me; a place of great struggle but also of great encounter. It is here in the great silence that I can see not only my wounds and limitations, but also the truth of who I really am.

"The purpose of life," said Rilke, "is to be defeated by greater and greater things." How deeply this rings true for me. For as I write these words my son and I are being evicted from our little cabin in the woods of Norfolk. Every other weekend I visited my son here for nearly twenty years. It not only provided me with shelter, but a home to offer my son. Then, from out of nowhere, we received a letter informing us that due to planned regeneration of the area our little home would no longer be welcome and would be towed away.

The letting go of our beloved tin house in the woods was unbearably painful. Each picture we took down together felt like a blasphemous act. An insult to the love and tenderness that so joyfully came together to make this place such a beautiful home for us both. Yet such a letting go is a true rite of passage for us both. For my son, at age twenty, it marks the end of his childhood and his transition into manhood. For myself, it marks not just the end of our home, with all its wonderful memories, but it also marks the end of my twenty-year experiment of living in the wild. For I came to love this little patch of woodland as if it was my own, and my worn and shabby tin hut became like an extension of my very own body.

At times I wish I could press the pause button on loss, just so that I could catch my breath at least. But time and time again I am reminded that loss is as much a part of life as the interplay of light and dark that make up each day.

Befriending loss and loneliness has enabled me to integrate the light and dark elements within myself, enabling me to cross that abyss which separated me from my own personal suffering and the suffering of the world.

A deeper faith has grown in me through the purifying fire of grief. A faith that cannot so much be questioned but lived. And at the centre of this faith is love.

References

These are listed in the order in which they appear in the book.

Dedication
Dostoevsky, F. (2016 [1879]) *The Brothers Karamazov,* Book VI Chapter 2c, Toronto, Aegitas Publishing

Acknowledgements
Dass, R. [online]. Available at https://www.goodreads.com/quotes/40582-we-re-all-just-walking-each-other-home (Accessed 6 October 2020)

Epigraph
Rilke, R. M. (1995 [1922–26]) Ah, not to be cut off, *Ahead of All Parting: The Selected Poetry and Prose of Rainer Maria Rilke,* (trans. S. Mitchell), New York, Modern Library, Random House Inc.

Introduction
O'Donohue, J. (2004) *Divine Beauty: The Invisible Embrace,* New York, Bantam, p. 35

Meditation 1: Loneliness
Rilke, R. M. (1996 [1905]) *Rilke's Book of Hours: Love Poems to God,* The Book of Pilgrimage, II.1, (trans. A. Barrows and J. Macy), New York, Riverhead Books, p. 95

Meditation 2: Stumbling into grace
Rilke, R. M. (1996 [1905]) *Rilke's Book of Hours: Love Poems to God,* The Book of Pilgrimage, II.12, (trans. A. Barrows and J. Macy), New York, Riverhead Books, p. 113
Rilke, R. M. (1996 [1905]) The Beauty of You, *Rilke's Book of Hours:*

The Book of Pilgrimage, II.34, *Love Poems to God,* (trans. A. Barrows and J. Macy), New York, Riverhead Books, p. 124

Meditation 3: Storehouses

Rilke, R. M. (1996 [1905]) *Rilke's Book of Hours: Love Poems to God,* The Book of Pilgrimage, II.2, (trans. A. Barrows and J. Macy), New York, Riverhead Books, p. 112

Meditation 4: The great storm

Rilke, R.M. (1918 [1902]), Presaging, *Poems, Rainer Maria Rilke,* The Book of Pictures, (trans from German by J. Lemont 1918, Fairford, Echo Library; Reprint of an Earlier ed. Edition (2017), [online] Available at https://en.m.wikisource.org/wiki/Poems_of_Rainer_Maria_Rilke_(1918) (Accessed September 2020)

Thich Nhat Hanh, [online] Available at https://www.goodreads.com/quotes/3228751-interbeing-if-you-are-a-poet-you-will-see-clearly (Accessed 20 March 2020)

Julian of Norwich (1980 [1373]), *Enfolded in Love,* (ed. Robert Llewellyn, trans. Sheila Upjohn), London, Darton, Longman and Todd Ltd., p.15

Meditation 5: Embracing struggle

Rilke, R. M. (1918 [1905], I Live My Life in Circles, *Poems, Rainer Maria Rilke,* The Book of Hours: The Book of a Monk's Life, (trans from German by J. Lemont 1918) Fairford, Echo Library; Reprint of an Earlier ed. Edition (2017) [online] Available at https://en.m.wikisource.org/wiki/Poems_of_Rainer_Maria_Rilke_(1918) (Accessed 1 September 2020)

Berry, W. (2011 [1983]) The Real Work, *Standing by Words: Essays,* Berkeley, CA, Counterpoint Press [online] Available at https://www.goodreads.com/quotes/166119-it-may-be-that-when-we-no-longer-know-what (Accessed 20 March 2020)

Jacob wrestling with the angel, Genesis 32.22–32, *Holy Bible, New International Version,* London, Hodder & Stoughton

Meditation 6: Between two worlds
Rilke, R. M. (1996 [1905]) *Rilke's Book of Hours: Love Poems to God,* The Book of Pilgrimage, II.1, (trans. A. Barrows and J Macy), New York, Riverhead Books, p. 95

Meditation 7: An undefended life
Rilke, R. M. (1918 [1905]), I Love My Life's Dark Hours, *Poems, Rainer Maria Rilke,* The Book of Hours: The Book of a Monk's Life, (trans from German by J. Lemont 1918), Fairford, Echo Library; Reprint of an Earlier ed. Edition (2017) [online] Available at https://en.m.wikisource.org/wiki/Poems_of_Rainer_Maria_Rilke_(1918) (Accessed 1 September 2020)

Hazrat Inayat Khan, [online] Available at Goodreads, https://www.goodreads.com/quotes/7168505-god-breaks-the-heart-again-and-again-and-again-until (Accessed 6 October 2020)

Meditation 8: Excuse me sir, I believe...
Rilke, R. M. (1996 [1905]), *Rilke's Book of Hours: Love Poems to God,* The Book of Pilgrimage, II.2, (trans. A. Barrows and J. Macy), New York, Riverhead Books, p. 98

Chesterton, G. K. (reprint 2016) [1908]), *All Things Considered,* Redditch, Read Books Ltd [online] Available at https://books.google.co.uk/books?id=9QHcCwAAQBAJ&dq=all+things+-considered&source=gbs_navlinks_s (Accessed 20 March 2020)

Meditation 9: An amends to yourself
Rilke, R. M. (1918 [1905]), In Cassocks Clad, *Poems, Rainer Maria Rilke,* The Book of Hours: The Book of a Monk's Life, I.3, (trans from German by J. Lemont 1918), Fairford, Echo Library; Reprint of an Earlier ed. Edition (2017) [online]

Available at https://en.m.wikisource.org/wiki/Poems_of_ Rainer_Maria_Rilke_(1918) (Accessed 1 September 2020)

Rilke, R. M. (2011 [1929]), *Letters to a Young Poet*, (trans. C. Louth, ed.), London, Penguin Classics, p. 27

Meditation 10: A dignified life

Rilke, R. M. (2006 [1905]), (trans. A. Barrows and J. Macy), *Rilke's Book of Hours: Love Poems to God*, The Book of a Monastic Life, I.13, New York, Riverhead Books, p. 59

Blake, W. *Auguries of Innocence*, [online] Available at Goodreads https://www.goodreads.com/quotes/7186590-joy-and-woe-are-woven-fine-a-clothing-for-the (Accessed 19 March 2020)

Meditation 11: Touched by life

Rilke, R. M. (1996 [1905]), *Rilke's Book of Hours: Love Poems to God*, The Book of a Monastic Life, I.1, (trans. A. Barrows and J. Macy), 2006, New York, Riverhead Books, p. 47

Rilke, R. M. (1996 [1905]), *Rilke's Book of Hours: Love Poems to God*, The Book of a Monastic Life, I.50, (trans. A. Barrows and J. Macy), New York, Riverhead Books, p. 83

Jesus washing his disciples' feet, 1995, John 13.4–17 *Holy Bible, New International Version* London, Hodder & Stoughton

Meditation 12: You, my own deep soul

Rilke, R. M. (1996 [1905]), *Rilke's Book of Hours: Love Poems to God*, The Book of a Monastic Life, I.39, (trans. A. Barrows and J. Macy), New York, Riverhead Books, p. 77

Blake, W. [1789] The Little Black Boy, *Songs of Innocence*, [online] Available at https://www.poetryfoundation.org/poems/43671/the-little-black-boy (Accessed 20 March 2020)

Baba, M. 1987, *Discourses*, 7th ed. p. 8–9, Eventually it transforms everyone, [online] Available at https://www.avatarmeherbaba.org/erics/catchit.html (Accessed 6 October 2020)

Meditation 13: Thou Art in calm and storm

Rilke, R. M. (1918 [1905]), All Those Who Seek Thee, *Poems, Rainer Maria Rilke,* The Book of Pilgrimage, (trans from German by J. Lemont 1918) Fairford, Echo Library; Reprint of an Earlier ed. Edition (2017) [online] Available at https://en.m.wikisource.org/wiki/Poems_of_Rainer_Maria_Rilke_(1918) (Accessed 1 September 2020)

Rilke, R. M. (2015 [1908]), Buddha in Glory, *Ahead of All Parting: The Selected Poetry and Prose of Rainer Maria Rilke,* (trans. S. Mitchell), New York, Random House Publishing Group

Merton, T. (2011), *The Hidden Ground of Love: Letters,* New York, Farrar, Straus and Giroux, [online] Available at https://books.google.co.uk/books?id=7j7lSkDrcwC&dq=The&q=you+-may+have+to+fact+the+fact+that+your+work#v=snippet&q=you%20may%20have%20to%20face%20the%20fact%20that%20your%20work&f=true (Accessed 6 October 2020)

Meditation 14: Tenderising of the soul

Rilke, R. M. [online] Available at, https://www.beliefnet.com/quotes/angel/r/rainer-maria-rilke/the-angels-love-our-tears-leaving-they-dry-our.aspx (Accessed 6 October 2020)

Franck, F. (1999), *A Little Compendium on that which matters,* vol XII, no. 5 [online] Available at https://friendsofsilence.net/quote/1999/05/when-heart-weeps-what-it-has-lost-spirit-laughs-what-it-has-gained (Accessed 6 October 2020) [Sufi Saying]

Mendel, M. (1787–1859) [online] Available at https://www.voices-visions.org/content/poster/collection-poster-rabbi-menachem-mendel-kotzk-michael-peters (Accessed 6 October 2020)

Mendel, M. (1787–1859), (Commentary Erica Brown) [online] Available at https://www.voices-visions.org/content/poster/

collection-poster-rabbi-menachem-mendel-kotzk-michael-peters (Accessed 20 March 2020)

Meditation 15: By way of loss

Rilke, R. M. (1918 [1902]) Music, *Poems, Rainer Maria Rilke,* The Book of Pictures, (trans from German by J. Lemont 1918), Fairford, Echo Library; Reprint of an Earlier ed. Edition (2017) [online] Available at https://en.m.wikisource.org/wiki/Poems_of_Rainer_Maria_Rilke_(1918) (Accessed 1 September 2020)

Appleton, G. (adapted by Jim Cotter), [online] Available at https://www.churchtimes.co.uk/articles/2013/30-august/faith/prayer-for-the-week/prayer-for-the-week (Accessed 7 October 2020)

Meditation 16: An embodied life

Rilke, R. M. [online] Available at https://www.brainpickings.org/2014/08/07/rilke-on-body-and-soul/ (Accessed 1 September 2020)

Meditation 17: As gently as a feather

Rilke, R. M. (1996 [1905]), *Rilke's Book of Hours: Love Poems to God,* The Book of Poverty and Death, III.28, (trans. A. Barrows and J. Macy), New York, Riverhead Books, p. 145

Tzu, L. [online] Available at https://www.goodreads.com/quotes/7918-if-you-do-not-change-direction-you-may-end-up (Accessed 6 October 2020)

Rilke, R. M. (2011 [1929]), *Letters to a Young Poet,* (trans. C. Louth, ed.), London, Penguin Classics, p. 6

Meditation 18: What used to be a hindrance

Rilke, R. M. (1996 [1905]), *Rilke's Book of Hours: Love Poems to God,* The Book of a Monastic Life, II.1, (trans. A. Barrows and J. Macy), New York, Riverhead Books, p. 47

Laird, M. (2011), *A Sunlit Absence: Silence, Awareness, and Contemplation,* New York, Oxford University Press, [Meister Eckhart]

Meditation 19: The ear of your heart

Rilke, R. M. (1918 [1905]), Thou Anxious One, *Poems, Rainer Maria Rilke:* The Book of Hours, (trans from German by J. Lemont 1918), Fairford, Echo Library; Reprint of an Earlier ed. Edition (2017), [online] Available at https://en.m.wikisource. org/wiki/Poems_of_Rainer_Maria_Rilke_(1918) (Accessed 1 September 2020)

Benedict of Nursia (2015 [516]), Prologue, *Saint Benedict's Rule for Monasteries,* (trans. from the Latin L G Doyle.) Collegeville, Minnesota, The Liturgical Press

Anonymous (2017 [1884]), *The Way of a Pilgrim: Candid Tales of a Wanderer to His Spiritual Father,* (trans. A. Zaranko, ed. A. Louth), London, Penguin Random House

Laird, M. S. (2019), *An Ocean of Light: Contemplation, Transformation, and Liberation* New York, Oxford University Press, p. 159

Meditation 20: A radical dependency

Rilke, R. M. (1996 [1905]), *Rilke's Book of Hours: Love Poems to God.* The Book of Pilgrimage, II.2, (trans. A. Barrows and J. Macy), New York, Riverhead Books, p. 98

Talbot, J. M. (2013), *The Jesus Prayer: A Cry for Mercy, A Path of Renewal,* Illinois, InterVarsity Press

Bloom, A. [online] Available at Goodreads https://www. goodreads.com/quotes/8892938-st-john-chrysostom-said-find-the-door-of-your-heart (Accessed 6 October 2020), [St John Chrysostom]

Meditation 21: Home will bring you home

Rilke, R. M. (1996 [1905]), *Rilke's Book of Hours: Love Poems to*

God, The Book of a Monastic Life, I.50, (trans. A. Barrows and J Macy), New York, Riverhead Books, p. 83

Rilke, R. M. (1981), (trans. R. Bly), A Walk, *Selected Poems of Rainer Maria Rilke*, [online] Available at https://www.poetry-chaikhana.com/blog/2016/01/12/rainer-maria-rilke-a-walk/ (Accessed 6 October 2020), New York, Harper & Row

Meditation 22: When curiosity becomes stronger than fear

Rilke, R. M. (1996 [1905]), *Rilke's Book of Hours: Love Poems to God*, The Book of a Monastic Life, I,59(trans. A. Barrows and J. Macy), New York, Riverhead Books p. 88

Schaller, G. [online] Available at https://jackkornfield.com/awakening-buddha-wisdom-difficulties/ (Accessed 6 October 2020)

Ackerman, D. (1991), *A Natural History of the Senses*, New York, Vintage Books

Meditation 23: The sacrament of tenderness

Rilke, R. M. (1996 [1905]), *Rilke's Book of Hours: Love Poems to God*, The Book of Poverty and Death, III.19, (trans. A. Barrows and J. Macy), New York, Riverhead Books, p. 143

Meditation 24: Until it takes

Rilke, R. M. (1996 [1905]), *Rilke's Book of Hours: Love Poems to God*, The Book of Pilgrimage, II.2, (trans. A. Barrows and J. Macy), New York, Riverhead Books, p. 98

Tagore, R. (2018 [1910]), *Gitanjali, A Collection of Nobel Prize Winning Poems*. Chapter 29 New Delhi, General Press, [online] Available at https://books.google.co.uk/books?id=opsEDAAAQBAJ&pg=PP7&dq=Gitanjali+chapter+29&hl=en&sa=X&ved=2a-hUKEwjc9IXy2bTsAhUgVBUIHVURA3sQ6AEwA-HoECAYQAg#v=onepage&q=Gitanjali%20chapter%2029&f=false (Accessed 6 October 2020)

Meditation 25: Intensified sky

Rilke, R. M. (1995 [1922–26]) Ah, not to be cut off, *Ahead of All Parting: The Selected Poetry and Prose of Rainer Maria Rilke,* (trans. S. Mitchell), New York, Modern Library, Random House Inc.

Meditation 26: Walking in the light

Rilke, R. M. (1918 [1905]), By Day Thou Art The Legend and The Dream, *Poems, Rainer Maria Rilke,* The Book of Pilgrimage, (trans from German by J. Lemont 1918), Fairford, Echo Library; Reprint of an Earlier ed. Edition (2017) [online] Available at https://en.m.wikisource.org/wiki/Poems_of_Rainer_Maria_Rilke_(1918) (Accessed 1 September 2020)
The Road to Emmaus, Luke 24.13–35, *Holy Bible, New International Version,* London, Hodder & Stoughton

Meditation 27: A graceful elegance

Rilke, R. M. (1996 [1905]), *Rilke's Book of Hours: Love Poems to God,* The Book of a Monastic Life, I.60, (trans. A. Barrows and J Macy), New York, Riverhead Books, p. 89
Hillesum, E. (1996 [1941–1943]), *Etty Hillesum: An Interrupted Life and Letters from Westerbork,* (trans. A. J. Pomerans), New York, Owl Books
O'Donohue, J. (2003), *Divine Beauty: The Invisible Embrace,* London, Bantam Press

Meditation 28: A most tender knowing

Rilke, R. M. (1996 [1905]), *Rilke's Book of Hours: Love Poems to God,* The Book of a Monastic Life, I.29, (trans. A. Barrows and J. Macy), New York, Riverhead Books, p. 71
Weil, S. (2002 [1947]), *Gravity and Grace,* New York, Routledge Classics
Rumi [online] Available at https://www.goodreads.com/quotes/103315-the-wound-is-the-place-where-the-light-

enters-you (Accessed 19 March 2020)

Meditation 29: Writing as a way of being
Rilke, R. M. (1918 [1902]), Initiation, *Poems, Rainer Maria Rilke,* The Book of Pictures, (trans from German by J. Lemont 1918), Fairford, Echo Library; Reprint of an Earlier ed. Edition (2017), [online] Available at https://en.m.wikisource.org/wiki/Poems_of_Rainer_Maria_Rilke_(1918) (Accessed 1 September 2020)
Rilke, R. M. (1929), *Letters to a Young Poet,* [online] Available at https://www.goodreads.com/quotes/1243-find-out-the-reason-that-commands-you-to-write-see#:%7E:text=%E2%80%9CFind (Accessed 8 October 2020)
Rilke, R. M. (2011 [1929]), *Letters to a Young Poet,* Introduction, (trans. C. Louth, ed.), London, Penguin Classics, p. xx

Meditation 30: Heart-Work
Rilke, R. M. (1918 [1905]), Extinguish my eyes, *Poems, Rainer Maria Rilke,* The Book of Pilgrimage, (trans from German by J. Lemont 1918), Fairford, Echo Library; Reprint of an Earlier ed. Edition (2017), [online] Available at https://en.m.wikisource.org/wiki/Poems_of_Rainer_Maria_Rilke_(1918) (Accessed 1 September 2020)
Rilke, R. M. (2011 [1929]) *Letters to a Young Poet* [online] Available at https://www.goodreads.com/quotes/563483-i-beg-you-to-have-patience-with-everything-unresolved-in (Accessed 1 September 2020)

Meditation 31: Being love
Rilke, R. M. (1918 [1907]), Love song, *Poems, Rainer Maria Rilke,* New Poems, (trans from German by J. Lemont 1918), Fairford, Echo Library; Reprint of an Earlier ed. Edition (2017) [online] Available at https://en.m.wikisource.org/wiki/Poems_of_Rainer_Maria_Rilke_(1918) (Accessed 1 September 2020)

Rilke, R. M. (2011 [1929]), *Letters to a Young Poet*, [online] Available at https://www.brainyquote.com/quotes/rainer_maria_rilke_164598 (Accessed 8 October 2020)

Bourgeault, C. (2010), *The Meaning of Mary Magdalene: Discovering the Woman at the Heart of Christianity*, Colorado, Shambhala, p. 112

Meditation 32: An exquisite risk

Rilke, R. M. (1996 [1905]), *Rilke's Book of Hours: Love Poems to God,* The Book of a Monastic Life, I.2, (trans. A. Barrows and J. Macy), New York, Riverhead Books, p. 48

Blackstone, J. (2008), *The Enlightenment Process: A Guide to Embodied Spiritual Awakening* (Revised and Expanded), Massachusetts, Paragon House

Nepo, M. (2000), *The Book of Awakening: Having the Life You Want by Being Present to the Life You Have,* Conari Press, Massachusetts, p. 158

Meditation 33: Farewell

Rilke, R. M. (1996 [1905]), *Rilke's Book of Hours: Love Poems to God,* The Book of Poverty and Death, III.7, (trans. A. Barrows and J. Macy), New York, Riverhead Books, p. 132

Meditation 34: The Serenity Prayer

Rilke, R. M. (1996 [1905]), Thanksgiving, *Rilke's Book of Hours: Love Poems to God*, The Book of a Monastic Life, I.62, (trans. A. Barrows and J. Macy), New York, Riverhead Books, p. 147

Niebuhr, R. (Attributed to) [1955], *The Serenity Prayer*, [online] Available at http://www.aahistory.com/prayer.html (Accessed 20 September 2020)

Lewis, C. S. [online] Available at https://www.goodreads.com/quotes/1005539-i-pray-because-i-can-t-help-myself-i-pray-because (Accessed 20 March 2020)

Chah, A. [online] Available at https://quotes.justdharma.com/

letting-go-ajahn-chah/ (Accessed 20 March 2020)

Meditation 35: I love you, gentlest of Ways

Rilke, R. M. (1996 [1905]), *Rilke's Book of Hours: Love Poems to God*, The Book of a Monastic Life, I.25 (trans. A. Barrows and J. Macy), New York, Riverhead Books, p. 70

Pennington, I. (2013 [1667]), *Quaker Faith and Practice: Fifth edition*. Chapter 10, Section 10.01., London, Quaker Books

Meditation 36: A beautiful practice

Rilke, R. M. (1996 [1905]), *Rilke's Book of Hours: Love Poems to God*, The Book of a Monastic Life, I.21 (trans. A. Barrows and J. Macy), New York, Riverhead Books, p. 67

Thich Nhat Hanh, (2008), *Understanding Our Mind*, California, Parallax Press

Meditation 37: The Way of a Pilgrim

Rilke, R. M. (1996 [1905]), *Rilke's Book of Hours: Love Poems to God*, The Book of a Monastic Life, I.25 (trans. A. Barrows and J. Macy), New York, Riverhead Books, p. 70

Anonymous (2017 [1884]), *The Way of a Pilgrim: Candid Tales of a Wanderer to His Spiritual Father,* (trans. A. Zaranko, ed. A. Louth), London, Penguin Random House, p. 3

Meditation 38: The Winds of Homecoming

Rilke, R. M. (1995 [1922–26]), Ah, not to be cut off, *Ahead of All Parting: The Selected Poetry and Prose of Rainer Maria Rilke,* (trans. S. Mitchell), New York, Modern Library, Random House Inc.

Lindbergh, A. M. (1992 [1955]), *Gift from the Sea*, London, Chatto and Windus Ltd, [online] Available at https://www. brainyquote.com/quotes/anne_morrow_lindbergh_133336 (Accessed 20 April 2020)

Meditation 39: A God hidden in Tenderness

Rilke, R. M. (1918 [1907]), Offering, *Poems, Rainer Maria Rilke, New Poems*, (trans from German by J. Lemont 1918), Fairford, Echo Library; Reprint of an Earlier ed. Edition (2017), [online] Available at https://en.m.wikisource.org/wiki/Poems_of_Rainer_Maria_Rilke_(1918) (Accessed 1 September 2020)

(1995), John 13.8, *Holy Bible, New International Version*, London, Hodder & Stoughton, [Jesus]

(1995), John 13.15, *Holy Bible, New International Version*, London, Hodder & Stoughton, [Jesus]

Meditation 40: A twilight dwelling

Rilke, R. M. (1996 [1905]), *Rilke's Book of Hours: Love Poems to God*, The Book of a Monastic Life, I.38 (trans. A. Barrows and J. Macy), New York, Riverhead Books, p. 76

Saunders, A. [online] Available at https://www.goodreads.com/quotes/tag/misattributed-john-lennon (Accessed 19 April 2020)

Meditation 41: Unlearning your way back to God

Rilke, R. M. (1996 [1905]), *Rilke's Book of Hours: Love Poems to God*, The Book of a Monastic Life, I.16 (trans. A. Barrows and J. Macy), New York, Riverhead Books, p. 63

Meditation 42: That which is wide and timeless

Rilke, R. M. (1996 [1905]), *Rilke's Book of Hours: Love Poems to God*, The Book of a Monastic Life, I.5 (trans. A. Barrows and J. Macy), New York, Riverhead Books, p. 51

Butler, A. (1991 [1273]), Lives of the Saints, (revised Thurston and Attwater) San Francisco, Harper Collins, [online] Available at https://www.catholic.com/qa/when-st-thomas-aquinas-likened-his-work-to-straw-was-that-a-retraction-of-what-he-wrote (Accessed 20 April 2020) [St Thomas Aquinas]

Rilke, R. M. (1996 [1905]), *Rilke's Book of Hours: Love Poems to*

God, The Book of Pilgrimage, II.12, (trans. A. Barrows and J. Macy), New York, Riverhead Books, pp. 113–14

Meditation 43: Solitude as a way of being

Rilke, R. M. (1918 [1902]), Solitude, *Poems, Rainer Maria Rilke, The Book of Pictures,* (trans from German by J Lemont 1918), Fairford, Echo Library; Reprint of an Earlier ed. Edition (2017), [online] Available at https://en.m.wikisource.org/wiki/Poems_of_Rainer_Maria_Rilke_(1918),   (Accessed   1 September 2020)

Teilhard de Chardin, P. (2008 [1955]), *The Phenomenon of Man,* New York, Harper Perennial, [online] Available at https://www.goodreads.com/author/quotes/5387.Pierre_Teilhard_de_Chardin, (Accessed 20 April 2020)

Meditation 44: "Be" the mystery at the crossroads

Rilke, R. M. (1996 [1905]), *Rilke's Book of Hours: Love Poems to God,* The Book of a Monastic Life, I.39, (trans. A. Barrows and J. Macy), New York, Riverhead Books, p. 78

Rilke, R. M. Let This Darkness Be a Bell Tower, *Sonnets to Orpheus II,29,* (trans. J. Macy) [online] Available at https://onbeing.org/poetry/let-this-darkness-be-a-bell-tower/ (Accessed 20 September 2020)

Meditation 45: What has been whispered to you

Rilke, R. M. (1996 [1905]), *Rilke's Book of Hours: Love Poems to God,* The Book of a Monastic Life, I.18, (trans. A. Barrows and J. Macy), New York, Riverhead Books, p. 65

Teilhard de Chardin, P. (1962), [online] Available at https://catholicnetwork.us/2019/06/05/love-is-the-very-physical-structure-of-the-universe-on-giving-up-our-separation-superiority-privilege-and-control/#:~:text=Love%20is%20%E2%80%9Cthe%20very%20physical,privilege%20and%20control%20%E2%80%93%20CatholicNetwork.US, (Accessed

20 September 2020)

Nepo, M. (2005), *The Exquisite Risk: Daring to Live an Authentic Life*, New York, Harmony p. 188

Meditation 46: Prayer of the heart

Rilke, R. M. (1996 [1905]), *Rilke's Book of Hours: Love Poems to God*, The Book of a Monastic Life, I.51, (trans. A. Barrows and J. Macy), New York, Riverhead Books, p. 84

St Catherine of Siena (1347-1380), [online] Available at https://www.goodreads.com/quotes/243140-all-the-way-to-heaven-is-heaven-because-jesus-said (Accessed 20 September 2020)

Talbot, J. M. (2013), *The Jesus Prayer: A Cry for Mercy, A Path of Renewal*, Illinois, InterVarsity Press

Meditation 47: An anchored presence

Rilke, R. M. (1996 [1905]), *Rilke's Book of Hours: Love Poems to God*, The Book of a Monastic Life, I.19, (trans. A. Barrows and J. Macy), New York, Riverhead Books, p. 66

Julian of Norwich (1980 [1373]), *Enfolded in Love*, (ed. Robert Llewellyn, trans. Sheila Upjohn), London, Darton, Longman and Todd Ltd., p. 15

Meditation 48: A gathered silence

Rilke, R. M. (1996 [1905]), *Rilke's Book of Hours: Love Poems to God*, The Book of a Monastic Life, I.49, (trans. A. Barrows and J. Macy), New York, Riverhead Books, p. 82

(2009), *Quaker Faith and Practice, Fourth Edition*, Chapter 27 Section 27.27, London: Quaker Peace and Service, [Isaac Penington, 1616–1679]

Meditation 49: So tender

Rilke, R. M. (1918 [1902]), Death, *Poems, Rainer Maria Rilke*, The Book of Pictures, (trans from German by J. Lemont 1918), Fairford, Echo Library; Reprint of an Earlier ed. Edition

(2017) [online] Available at https://en.m.wikisource.org/wiki/Poems_of_Rainer_Maria_Rilke_(1918) (Accessed 1 September 2020)

Meditation 50: Rearranged by life

Rilke, R. M. (1996 [1905]), *Rilke's Book of Hours: Love Poems to God*, The Book of Pilgrimage, II.12, (trans. A. Barrows and J. Macy), New York, Riverhead Books, p. 114

Rilke, R. M. (2011 [1929]), *Letters to a Young Poet*, [online] Available at https://www.goodreads.com/quotes/9371-the-purpose-of-life-is-to-be-defeated-by-greater (Accessed 19 April 2020)

Further Reading

Alexander, F. M. (1985 [1932]), *The Use of the Self*, London, Victor Gollancz

Durham, G. (2011), *Being a Quaker: A Guide for Newcomers*, London, Quaker Quest

(2013), *Quaker Faith and Practice, The book of Christian discipline of the Yearly Meeting of the Religious Society of Friends (Quakers) in Britain, Fifth Edition*, London: Quaker Books

Julian of Norwich (1998 [1373]), *Revelations of Divine Love*, (trans E. Spearing), London

Ramirez, J. (2017), *Julian of Norwich (A very brief history)*, SPCK

Saint-Exupéry, A. de (1995 [1943]), *The Little Prince*, (trans. I. Testot-Ferry), Ware, Hertfordshire, Wordsworth Editions Limited

Thich Nhat Hanh, (1975), *The Miracle of Mindfulness*, Boston, Mass.

Vanier, J. (2004), *Drawn into the Mystery of Jesus Through the Gospel of John*, Mahwah, NJ, Paulist Press

Copyright Acknowledgements

The author is grateful for permission from the following:

Kröller-Müller Museum for the use of *Avenue of Poplars at Sunset* Vincent van Gogh.

Kent Ambler for the four woodcuts © 2015, 2015, 2019, 2020.

Aegitas for the quotation by Dostoevsky.

Anita Barrows and Joanna Macy for the use of their translations from *Rilke's Book of Hours, Love Poems to God.* © 1996.

Echo Library for the use of their 2017 reprint of the 1918 edition of *Poems of Rainer Maria Rilke.*

Penguin, from *Letters to a Young Poet* by Rainer Maria Rilke Copyright translation © by Charlie Louth 2016 published by Penguin Classics 2016. Reproduced by permission of Penguin Books Ltd ©

Penguin Random House for Steven Mitchell's translation of Rilke's poem,

Ah, not to be cut off, from *Ahead of All Parting — The Selected Poetry and Prose of Rainer Maria Rilke.* © 1995. Permission pending.

RWW Books for the quotation by Mark Nepo from *The Book of Awakening: Having the Life You Want by Being Present to the Life You Have.*

Hodder & Stoughton, Headline Publishing, John Murray Press, Quercus, for the quotation by Mark Nepo from *The Book of Awakening: Having the Life You Want by Being Present to the Life You Have.*

Scripture quotations taken from the HOLY BIBLE, NEW INTERNATIONAL VERSION, Copyright © 1973, 1978, 1984 by International Bible Society. Used by permission of Hodder & Stoughton Ltd, a member of the Hodder Headline Plc Group. All rights reserved. "NIV" is a registered trademark of International Bible Society. UK trademark number 1448790.

The author has made every reasonable effort to contact the copyright owners of the quotations reproduced in this book. He invites copyright holders to contact him direct in the cases where he has been unsuccessful.

About the Author

Christopher Goodchild is an Ignatian-trained Spiritual Director, Alexander Technique Teacher and author of *Unclouded by Longing* and *A Painful Gift: The Journey of a Soul with Autism*. He is a Quaker with a deep interest in Buddhist psychology, eastern philosophy, Advaita Vedanta and the Christian contemplative tradition. Based in London, he runs courses on Contemplative Spirituality and the Alexander Technique.

Diagnosed with autism in 2007, he is passionate about raising awareness of the enormous richness and diversity of the autism spectrum. An eloquent speaker, as ambassador for the National Autistic Society since 2010, he has featured in campaigns, broadcasts and interviews. His heart-rending account of life with autism formed the subject of his first book, *A Painful Gift: The Journey of a Soul with Autism* published by Darton, Longman and Todd in 2009.

Through his writing Christopher walks alongside his readers, not so much in his role as spiritual director, but as a fellow traveller, writing from a deeply human place of vulnerability and humility. He teaches us, not from some far distant place, but from personal experience, from the heart. His writing portrays his characteristic lyricism and tender-hearted, compassionate observations on the human condition. His loyal and often loving readership have followed him on his ongoing spiritual journey of unfolding and transformation over the past ten years. He loves walking in both remote and urban areas, and is known for writing from various locations around London and in the wild. He is passionate about non-league football, and is a keen supporter of Wealdstone, his childhood team. He has one son.

Previous Titles

A Painful Gift: The Journey of a Soul with Autism.
Illustrated by Julie Lonneman
Foreword by Jean Vanier
Endorsed by Gerard W Hughes, Donna Williams
and Bronwen Astor
Published by Darton Longman and Todd, 2009
ISBN 978 0 232 52758 2
This beautifully illustrated, moving and revelatory book
will inspire readers to see that it is often that which gives us
the deepest sorrow in life that can bring us the greatest joy.
"Welcome to my world. I have autism." But A Painful Gift
is not about my autism. It is about the struggle to be truly
ourselves in the world. To be fully human, to touch people and
to be touched by people in return.

*Unclouded by Longing: Meditations on Autism and being Present in
an Overwhelming World.*
Illustrated by Julie Lonneman
Foreword by Thomas Moore
Endorsed by Jennifer Kavanagh and Marion Partington
Published by Jessica Kingsley Publishers, 2017
ISBN 978 1 78592 122 3
"Truth waits for eyes unclouded by longing." Lao-
Tzu (poet and philosopher) In this collection of short,
contemplative, enlightening reflections, qualified spiritual
director and Quaker elder Chris Goodchild, inspired by
his own experiences, guides you through his spiritual and
philosophical journey to his truest and most peaceful self.
Don't read this book at a distance. Take it home, deep into
your heart. Be radicalised by it for your soul. Be fully in your
world, but follow the laws of a much vaster world, one that

can be known and cherished only mysteriously.
Extract from the foreword by Thomas Moore, Author of *Care of the Soul*.

About Sheila Cassidy

Sheila Cassidy is a British doctor, known for her work in the hospice movement, as a writer and as someone who, by publicising her own history as a torture survivor, drew attention to human rights abuse in Chile in the 1970s. A Roman Catholic, she has written a number of books on Christian subjects and has been involved with a number of charitable organisations such as patronage of The Prison Phoenix Trust.

Her books include:

Audacity to Believe (1977)

Sharing the Darkness: The Spirituality of Caring (1988)

Good Friday People (1991)

The Loneliest Journey (1995)

Made for Laughter (2006)

Confessions of a Lapsed Catholic (2010)

About the Artist

Kent Ambler was raised in NW Indiana about 30 miles from Chicago. After college he lived in New Mexico for seven years before settling in the upstate of South Carolina, in Greenville. He is a printmaker and painter. Woodcut prints are his medium of choice. He creates loosely cut prints based on everyday events and objects.

Kent was introduced to printmaking in college. The woodcut process instantly "clicked" with him. The other students and professor thought he had made woodcuts before as the process seemed completely natural for him.

In 1992, Kent graduated from Ball State University with a Bachelor of Fine Arts in Painting. He has been a full-time artist since 1997.

This is how Kent describes his work:

My work is autobiographical. It is derived from my life and surroundings, my observations. While the imagery in my art is generally subject or object oriented, the visual appearance of each piece is of most importance to me. I work from an aesthetic and intuitive approach rather than a conceptual one.

I try not to over-think or over-plan my work. I generally do my best work when my brain is "turned off" so to speak. I am inspired by the simplicity of idea and image addressed by genuine folk artists.

http://www.kentambler.net/

CHRISTIAN ALTERNATIVE
BOOKS

THE NEW OPEN SPACES

Throughout the two thousand years of Christian tradition there
have been, and still are, groups and individuals that exist in
the margins and upon the edge of faith. But in Christianity's
contrapuntal history it has often been these outcasts and
pioneers that have forged contemporary orthodoxy out
of former radicalism as belief evolves to engage with and
encompass the ever-changing social and scientific realities. Real
faith lies not in the comfortable certainties of the Orthodox,
but somewhere in a half-glimpsed hinterland on the dirt track
to Emmaus, where the Death of God meets the Resurrection,
where the supernatural Christ meets the historical Jesus,
and where the revolution liberates both the oppressed and
the oppressors.

Welcome to Christian Alternative... a space at the edge where
the light shines through.
If you have enjoyed this book, why not tell other readers by
posting a review on your preferred book site.
Recent bestsellers from Christian Alternative are:

Bread Not Stones
The Autobiography of An Eventful Life
Una Kroll
The spiritual autobiography of a truly remarkable woman
and a history of the struggle for ordination in the Church of
England.
Paperback: 978-1-78279-804-0 ebook: 978-1-78279-805-7

The Quaker Way
A Rediscovery
Rex Ambler
Although fairly well known, Quakerism is not well understood.
The purpose of this book is to explain how Quakerism works as
a spiritual practice.
Paperback: 978-1-78099-657-8 ebook: 978-1-78099-658-5

Blue Sky God
The Evolution of Science and Christianity
Don MacGregor
Quantum consciousness, morphic fields and blue-sky
thinking about God and Jesus the Christ.
Paperback: 978-1-84694-937-1 ebook: 978-1-84694-938-8

Celtic Wheel of the Year
Tess Ward
An original and inspiring selection of prayers combining
Christian and Celtic Pagan traditions, and interweaving their
calendars into a single pattern of prayer for every morning
and night of the year.
Paperback: 978-1-90504-795-6

Christian Atheist
Belonging without Believing
Brian Mountford
Christian Atheists don't believe in God but miss him: especially the transcendent beauty of his music, language, ethics, and community.
Paperback: 978-1-84694-439-0 ebook: 978-1-84694-929-6

Compassion Or Apocalypse?
A Comprehensible Guide to the Thoughts of René Girard
James Warren
How René Girard changes the way we think about God and the Bible, and its relevance for our apocalypse-threatened world.
Paperback: 978-1-78279-073-0 ebook: 978-1-78279-072-3

Diary Of A Gay Priest
The Tightrope Walker
Rev. Dr. Malcolm Johnson
Full of anecdotes and amusing stories, but the Church is still a dangerous place for a gay priest.
Paperback: 978-1-78279-002-0 ebook: 978-1-78099-999-9

Do You Need God?
Exploring Different Paths to Spirituality Even For Atheists
Rory J.Q. Barnes
An unbiased guide to the building blocks of spiritual belief.
Paperback: 978-1-78279-380-9 ebook: 978-1-78279-379-3

Readers of ebooks can buy or view any of these bestsellers by clicking on the live link in the title. Most titles are published in paperback and as an ebook. Paperbacks are available in traditional bookshops. Both print and ebook formats are available online.

Find more titles and sign up to our readers' newsletter at
http://www.johnhuntpublishing.com/christianity
Follow us on Facebook at
https://www.facebook.com/ChristianAlternative